WATCHERS OF THE SKY

THE TORCH-BEARERS

WATCHERS
OF THE SKY

BY

ALFRED NOYES

NEW YORK
FREDERICK A. STOKES COMPANY
PUBLISHERS

Republished 1971
Scholarly Press, Inc., 22929 Industrial Drive East
St. Clair Shores, Michigan 48080

Library of Congress Catalog Card Number: 72-131790
ISBN 0-403-00677-5

821.91
N952w

PREFATORY NOTE

This volume, while it is complete in itself, is also the first of a trilogy, the scope of which is suggested in the prologue. The story of scientific discovery has its own epic unity—a unity of purpose and endeavour—the single torch passing from hand to hand through the centuries; and the great moments of science when, after long labour, the pioneers saw their accumulated facts falling into a significant order—sometimes in the form of a law that revolutionised the whole world of thought—have an intense human interest, and belong essentially to the creative imagination of poetry. It is with these moments that my poem is chiefly concerned, not with any impossible attempt to cover the whole field or to make a new poetic system, after the Lucretian model, out of modern science.

The theme has been in my mind for a good many years; and the first volume, dealing with the "Watchers of the Sky," began to take definite shape during what was to me an unforgettable experience—the night I was privileged to spend on a summit of the Sierra Madre Mountains, when the first trial was made of the new 100-inch telescope. The prologue to this volume attempts to give a picture of that night, and to elucidate my own purpose.

The first tale in this volume plunges into the middle of things, with the revolution brought about by Copernicus; but, within the tale, partly by means of an incidental lyric, there is an attempt to give a bird's-eye view of what had gone before. The torch then passes to Tycho Brahe, who, driven into exile with his tables of the stars, at the very point of death hands them over to a young man named Kepler. Kepler, with their help, arrives at his own great laws, and corresponds with Galileo—the intensely human drama of whose life I have endeavoured to depict with more historical accuracy than can be attributed to much of the poetic literature that has gathered around his name. Too many writers have succumbed to the temptation of the cry, "e pur si muove!" It is, of course, rejected by every reliable historian, and was first attributed to Galileo a hundred years after his death. M. Ponsard, in his play on the subject, succumbed to the extent of making his final scéne end with Galileo "frappant du pied la terre," and crying, "pourtant elle tourne." Galileo's recantation was a far more subtle and tragically complicated affair than that. Even Landor succumbed to the easy method of making him display his entirely legendary scars to Milton. If these familiar pictures are not to be found in my poem, it may be well for me to assure the hasty reader that it is because I have endeavoured to present a more just picture. I have tried to suggest the complications of motive in this section by a series of letters passing between the characters chiefly concerned. There was, of course, a certain poetic significance in the legend of "e pur si muove"; and this significance I have endeavoured to retain without violating historical truth.

In the year of Galileo's death Newton was born, and the subsequent sections carry the story on to the modern observatory again. The form I have adopted is a development from that of an earlier book, *"Tales of the Mermaid Tavern,"* where certain poets and discoverers of another kind were brought together round a central idea, and their stories told in a combination of narrative and lyrical verse. "The Torch-Bearers" flowed all the more naturally into a similar form in view of the fact that Tycho Brahe, Kepler, and many other pioneers of science wrote a considerable num-

ber of poems. Those imbedded in the works
of Kepler—whose blazing and fantastic ge-
nius was, indeed, primarily poetic—are of
extraordinary interest. I was helped, too,
in the general scheme by those constant
meetings between science and poetry, of
which the most famous and beautiful are the
visit of Sir Henry Wotton to Kepler, and
the visit of Milton to Galileo in prison.

Even if science and poetry were as deadly
opposites as the shallow often affirm, the
method and scheme indicated above would
at least make it possible to convey something
of the splendour of the long battle for the
light in its most human aspect. Poetry has
its own precision of expression and, in mod-
ern times, it has been seeking more and
more for truth, sometimes even at the ex-
pense of beauty. It may be possible to
carry that quest a stage farther, to the point
where, in the great rhythmical laws of the
universe revealed by science, truth and
beauty are reunited. If poetry can do this,

it will not be without some value to science itself, and it will be playing its part in the reconstruction of a shattered world.

The passing of the old order of dogmatic religion has left the modern world in a strange chaos, craving for something in which it can unfeignedly believe, and often following will-o'-the-wisps. Forty years ago, Matthew Arnold prophesied that it would be for poetry, "where it is worthy of its high destinies," to help to carry on the purer fire, and to express in new terms those eternal ideas which must ever be the only sure stay of the human race. It is not within the province of science to attempt a post-Copernican justification of the ways of God to man; but, in the laws of nature revealed by science, and in "that grand sequence of events which"—as Darwin affirmed—"the mind refuses to accept as the result of blind chance," poetry may discover its own new grounds for the attempt. It is easy to assume that all hope and faith are shallow.

PREFATORY NOTE

It is even easier to practise a really shallow and devitalising pessimism. The modern annunciation that there is a skeleton an inch beneath the skin of man is neither new nor profound. Neither science nor poetry can rest there; and if, in this poem, an attempt is made to show that spiritual values are not diminished or overwhelmed by the "fifteen hundred universes" that passed in review before the telescope of Herschel, it is only after the opposite argument—so common and so easy to-day—has been faced; and only after poetry has at least endeavoured to follow the torch of science to its own deep-set boundary-mark in that immense darkness of Space and Time.

CONTENTS

PROLOGUE

THE OBSERVATORY

AT noon, upon the mountain's purple
height,
Above the pine-woods and the clouds it
shone
No larger than the small white dome of
shell
Left by the fledgling wren when wings are
born.
By night it joined the company of heaven,
And, with its constant light, became a
star.
A needle-point of light, minute, remote,
It sent a subtler message through the abyss,
Held more significance for the seeing eye
Than all the darkness that would blot it
out,
Yet could not dwarf it.

THE TORCH-BEARERS

        High in heaven it shone,
Alive with all the thoughts, and hopes, and
    dreams
Of man's adventurous mind.
        Up there, I knew
The explorers of the sky, the pioneers
Of science, now made ready to attack
That darkness once again, and win new
    worlds.
To-morrow night they hoped to crown the
    toil
Of twenty years, and turn upon the sky
The noblest weapon ever made by man.
War had delayed them. They had been
    drawn away
Designing darker weapons. But no gun
Could outrange this.

"To-morrow night"—so wrote their chief—
    "we try
Our great new telescope, the hundred-inch.
Your Milton's 'optic tube' has grown in
    power

WATCHERS OF THE SKY

Since Galileo, famous, blind, and old,
Talked with him, in that prison, of the
    sky.
We creep to power by inches. Europe
    trusts
Her 'giant forty' still. Even to-night
Our own old sixty has its work to do;
And now our hundred-inch . . . I hardly
    dare
To think what this new muzzle of ours
    may find.
Come up, and spend that night among the
    stars
Here, on our mountain-top. If all goes
    well,
Then, at the least, my friend, you'll see a
    moon
Stranger, but nearer, many a thousand mile
Than earth has ever seen her, even in
    dreams.
As for the stars, if seeing them were all,
Three thousand million new-found points
    of light

[3]

Is our rough guess. But never speak of
   this.
You know our press. They'd miss the one
   result
To flash 'three thousand millions' round
   the world."
To-morrow night! For more than twenty
   years,
They had thought and planned and worked.
   Ten years had gone,
One-fourth, or more, of man's brief work-
   ing life,
Before they made those solid tons of glass,
Their hundred-inch reflector, the clear
   pool,
The polished flawless pool that it must be
To hold the perfect image of a star.
And, even now, some secret flaw—none
   knew
Until to-morrow's test—might waste it all.
Where was the gambler that would stake
   so much,—

Time, patience, treasure, on a single throw?
The cost of it,—they'd not find that again,
Either in gold or life-stuff! All their youth
Was fuel to the flame of this one work.
Once in a lifetime to the man of science,
Despite what fools believe his ice-cooled
    blood,
There comes this drama.
                If he fails, he fails
Utterly. He at least will have no time
For fresh beginnings. Other men, no
    doubt,
Years hence, will use the footholes that he
    cut
In those precipitous cliffs, and reach the
    height,
But he will never see it."
                So for me,
The light words of that letter seemed to
    hide
The passion of a lifetime, and I shared
The crowning moment of its hope and fear.

THE TORCH-BEARERS

Next day, through whispering aisles of
    palm we rode
Up to the foot-hills, dreaming desert-hills
That to assuage their own delicious drought
Had set each tawny sun-kissed slope ablaze
With peach and orange orchards.
                    Up and up,
Along the thin white trail that wound and
    climbed
And zig-zagged through the grey-green
    mountain sage,
The car went crawling, till the shining
    plain
Below it, like an airman's map, unrolled.
Houses and orchards dwindled to white
    specks
In midget cubes and squares of tufted green.
Once, as we rounded one steep curve, that
    made
The head swim at the canyoned gulf be-
    low,
We saw through thirty miles of lucid air
Elvishly small, sharp as a crumpled petal

[6]

WATCHERS OF THE SKY

Blown from the stem, a yard away, a sail
Lazily drifting on the warm blue sea.
Up for nine miles along that spiral trail
Slowly we wound to reach the lucid
    height
Above the clouds, where that white dome
    of shell,
No wren's now, but an eagle's, took the flush
Of dying day. The sage-brush all died
    out,
And all the southern growths, and round
    us now,
Firs of the north, and strong, storm-rooted
    pines
Exhaled a keener fragrance; till, at last,
Reversing all the laws of lesser hills,
They towered like giants round us. Dark-
    ness fell
Before we reached the mountain's naked
    height.

Over us, like some great cathedral dome,
The observatory loomed against the sky;

THE TORCH-BEARERS

And the dark mountain with its headlong
    gulfs
Had lost all memory of the world below;
For all those cloudless throngs of glitter-
    ing stars
And all those glimmerings where the abyss
    of space
Is powdered with a milky dust, each grain
A burning sun, and every sun the lord
Of its own darkling planets,—all those
    lights
Met, in a darker deep, the lights of earth,
Lights on the sea, lights of invisible towns,
Trembling and indistinguishable from stars,
In those black gulfs around the mountain's
    feet.
Then, into the glimmering dome, with bated
    breath,
We entered, and, above us, in the gloom
Saw that majestic weapon of the light
Uptowering like the shaft of some huge gun
Through one arched rift of sky.
              Dark at its base

With naked arms, the crew that all day
    long
Had sweated to make ready for this night
Waited their captain's word.
            The switchboard shone
With elfin lamps of white and red, and
    keys
Whence, at a finger's touch, that monstrous
    tube
Moved like a creature dowered with life
    and will,
To peer from deep to deep.
            Below it pulsed
The clock-machine that slowly, throb by
    throb,
Timed to the pace of the revolving earth,
Drove the titanic muzzle on and on,
Fixed to the chosen star that else would
    glide
Out of its field of vision.
            So, set free
Balanced against the wheel of time, it
    swung,

[9]

Or rested, while, to find new realms of sky
The dome that housed it, like a moon re-
    volved,
So smoothly that the watchers hardly knew
They moved within; till, through the glim-
    mering doors,
They saw the dark procession of the pines
Like Indian warriors, quietly stealing by.

Then, at a word, the mighty weapon dipped
Its muzzle and aimed at one small point of
    light
One seeming insignificant star.
                    The chief,
Mounting the ladder, while we held our
    breath,
Looked through the eye-piece.
              Then we heard him laugh
His thanks to God, and hide it in a jest.
"A prominence on Jupiter!"—
                    They laughed,
"What do you mean?"—"It's moving,"
    cried the chief,

They laughed again, and watched his glim-
    mering face
High overhead against that moving tower.
"Come up and see, then!"
                One by one they went,
And, though each laughed as he returned
    to earth,
Their souls were in their eyes.
              Then I, too, looked,
And saw that insignificant spark of light
Touched with new meaning, beautifully
    reborn,
A swimming world, a perfect rounded
    pearl,
Poised in the violet sky; and, as I gazed,
I saw a miracle,—right on its upmost edge
A tiny mound of white that slowly rose,
Then, like an exquisite seed-pearl, swung
    quite clear
And swam in heaven above its parent world
To greet its three bright sister-moons.
                   A moon,
Of Jupiter, no more, but clearer far

Than mortal eyes had seen before from
    earth,
O, beautiful and clear beyond all dreams
Was that one silver phrase of the starry
    tune
Which Galileo's "old discoverer" first
Dimly revealed, dissolving into clouds
The imagined fabric of our universe.
"Jupiter stands in heaven and will stand
Though all the sycophants bark at him," he
    cried,
Hailing the truth before he, too, went
    down,
Whelmed in the cloudy wreckage of that
    dream.

So one by one we looked, the men who
    served
Urania, and the men from Vulcan's forge.
A beautiful eagerness in the darkness lit
The swarthy faces that too long had missed
A meaning in the dull mechanic maze

Of labour on this blind earth, but found it
    now.
Though only a moment's wandering melody
Hopelessly far above, it gave their toil
Its only consecration and its joy.
There, with dark-smouldering eyes and
    naked throats,
Blue-dungareed, red-shirted, grimed and
    smeared
With engine-grease and sweat, they gath-
    ered round
The foot of that dim ladder; each mutter-
    ing low
As he came down, his wonder at what he
    saw
To those who waited,—a picture for the
    brush
Of Rembrandt, lighted only by the rift
Above them, where the giant muzzle
    thrust
Out through the dim arched roof, and slow-
    ly throbbed,

Against the slowly moving wheel of the
    earth,
Holding their chosen star.
                     There, like an elf,
Perched on the side of that dark slanting
    tower
The Italian mechanician watched the
    moons,
That Italy discovered.
                    One by one,
American, English, French, and Dutch,
    they climbed
To see the wonder that their own blind
    hands
Had helped to achieve.
            At midnight while they paused
To adjust the clock-machine, I wandered
    out
Alone, into the silence of the night.
The silence? On that lonely height I
    heard
Eternal voices;
For, as I looked into the gulf beneath,

WATCHERS OF THE SKY

Whence almost all the lights had vanished
    now,
The whole dark mountain seemed to have
    lost its earth
And to be sailing like a ship through
    heaven.
All round it surged the mighty sea-like
    sound
Of soughing pine-woods, one vast ebb and
    flow
Of absolute peace, aloof from all earth's
    pain,
So calm, so quiet, it seemed the cradle-
    song,
The deep soft breathing of the universe
Over its youngest child, the soul of man.
And, as I listened, that Æolian voice
Became an invocation and a prayer:
O you, that on your loftier mountain dwell
And move like light in light among the
    thoughts
Of heaven, translating our mortality
Into immortal song, is there not one

THE TORCH-BEARERS

Among you that can turn to music now
This long dark fight for truth? Not one to
    touch
With beauty this long battle for the light,
This little victory of the spirit of man
Doomed to defeat—for what was all we saw
To that which neither eyes nor soul could
    see?—
Doomed to defeat and yet unconquerable,
Climbing its nine miles nearer to the stars.
Wars we have sung. The blind, blood-
    boltered kings
Move with an epic music to their thrones.
Have you no song, then, of that nobler war?
Of those who strove for light, but could not
    dream
Even of this victory that they helped to
    win,
Silent discoverers, lonely pioneers,
Prisoners and exiles, martyrs of the truth
Who handed on the fire, from age to age;
Of those who, step by step, drove back
    the night

And struggled, year on year, for one more
    glimpse
Among the stars, of sovran law, their
    guide;
Of those who searching inward, saw the
    rocks
Dissolving into a new abyss, and saw
Those planetary systems far within,
Atoms, electrons, whirling on their way
To build and to unbuild our solid world;
Of those who conquered, inch by difficult
    inch,
The freedom of this realm of law for man;
Dreamers of dreams, the builders of our
    hope,
The healers and the binders up of wounds,
Who, while the dynasts drenched the world
    with blood,
Would in the still small circle of a lamp
Wrestle with death like Heracles of old
To save one stricken child.
                 Is there no song
To touch this moving universe of law

THE TORCH-BEARERS

With ultimate light, the glimmer of that
    great dawn
Which over our ruined altars yet shall
    break
In purer splendour, and restore mankind
From darker dreams than even Lucretius
    knew
To vision of that one Power which guides
    the world.
How should men find it? Only through
    those doors
Which, opening inward, in each separate
    soul
Give each man access to that Soul of all
Living within each life, not to be found
Or known, till, looking inward, each alone
Meets the unknowable and eternal God.

And there was one that moved like light
    in light
Before me there,—Love, human and divine,
That can exalt all weakness into power,—

Whispering, *Take this deathless torch of
    song* . . .
Whispering, but with such faith, that even
    I
Was humbled into thinking this might be
Through love, though all the wisdom of
    the world
Account it folly.
               Let my breast be bared
To every shaft, then, so that Love be still
My one celestial guide the while I sing
Of those who caught the pure Promethean
    fire
One from another, each crying as he went
    down
To one that waited, crowned with youth
    and joy,—
*Take thou the splendour, carry it out of
    sight
Into the great new age I must not know,
Into the great new realm I must not tread.*

I

COPERNICUS

THE neighbours gossiped idly at the
    door.
Copernicus lay dying overhead.
His little throng of friends, with startled
    eyes,
Whispered together, in that dark house of
    dreams,
From which by one dim crevice in the wall
He used to watch the stars.
              "His book has come
From Nuremberg at last; but who would
    dare
To let him see it now?"—
             "They have altered it!
Though Rome approved in full, this pref-
    ace, look,

Declares that his discoveries are a
    dream!"—
"He has asked a thousand times if it has
    come;
Could we tear out those pages?"—
                     "He'd suspect."—
"What shall be done, then?"—
                  "Hold it back awhile.
That was the priest's voice in the room
    above.
He may forget it.   Those last sacraments
May set his mind at rest, and bring him
    peace."—
Then, stealing quietly to that upper door,
They opened it a little, and saw within
The lean white deathbed of Copernicus
Who made our world a world without an
    end.
There, in that narrow room, they saw his
    face
Grey, seamed with thought, lit by a single
    lamp;
They saw those glorious eyes

Closing, that once had looked beyond the
    spheres
And seen our ancient firmaments dissolve
Into a boundless night.
                Beside him knelt
Two women, like bowed shadows. At his
    feet,
An old physician watched him. At his head,
The cowled Franciscan murmured, while
    the light
Shone faintly on the chalice.
                  All grew still.
The fragrance of the wine was like faint
    flowers,
The first breath of those far celestial
    fields. . . .

Then, like a dying soldier, that must leave
His last command to others, while the fight
Is yet uncertain, and the victory far,
Copernicus whispered, in a fevered dream,
"Yes, it is Death. But you must hold him
    back,

There, in the doorway, for a little while,
Until I know the work is rightly done.
Use all your weapons, doctor. I must live
To see and touch one copy of my book.
Have they not brought it yet?

                   They promised me
It should be here by nightfall.

                  One of you go
And hasten it. I can hold back
Death till dawn.

Have they not brought it yet?—from Nu-
    remberg.
Do not deceive me. I must know it safe,
Printed and safe, for other men to use.
I could die then. My use would be ful-
    filled.
What has delayed them? Will not some
    one go
And tell them that my strength is running
    out?
Tell them that book would be an angel's
    hand

THE TORCH-BEARERS

In mine, an easier pillow for my head,
A little lantern in the engulfing dark.
You see, I hid its struggling light so long
Under too small a bushel, and I fear
It may go out forever.   In the noon
Of life's brief day, I could not see the need
As now I see it, when the night shuts down.
I was afraid, perhaps, it might confuse
The lights that guide us for the souls of
    men.

But now I see three stages in our life.
At first, we bask contented in our sun
And take what daylight shows us for the
    truth.
Then we discover, in some midnight grief,
How all day long the sunlight blinded us
To depths beyond, where all our knowledge
    dies.
That's where men shrink, and lose their
    way in doubt.
Then, last, as death draws nearer, comes
    a night

In whose majestic shadow men see God,
Absolute Knowledge, reconciling all.
So, all my life I pondered on that
  scheme
Which makes this earth the centre of all
  worlds,
Lighted and wheeled around by sun and
  moon
And that great crystal sphere wherein men
  thought
Myriads of lesser stars were fixed like
  lamps,
Each in its place,—one mighty glittering
  wheel
Revolving round this dark abode of man.
Night after night, with even pace they
  moved,
Year after year, not altering by one point,
Their order, or their stations, those fixed
  stars
In that revolving firmament. The Plough
Still pointed to the Pole. Fixed in their
  sphere,

How else explain that vast unchanging
    wheel?
How, but by thinking all those lesser lights
Were huger suns, divided from our earth
By so immense a gulf that, if they moved
Ten thousand leagues an hour among them-
    selves,
It would not seem one hair's-breadth to
    our eyes.
Utterly inconceivable, I know;
And yet we daily kneel to boundless
    Power
And build our hope on that Infinitude.

This did not daunt me, then. Indeed, I
    saw
Light upon chaos. Many discordant
    dreams
Began to move in lucid music now.
For what could be more baffling than the
    thought
That those enormous heavens must circle
    earth

WATCHERS OF THE SKY

Diurnally—a journey that would need
Swiftness to which the lightning flash
    would seem
A white slug creeping on the walls of night;
While, if earth softly on her axle spun
One quiet revolution answered all.
It was our moving selves that made the
    sky
Seem to revolve. Have not all ages seen
A like illusion baffling half mankind
In life, thought, art? Men think, at every
    turn
Of their own souls, the very heavens have
    moved.

Light upon chaos, light, and yet more
    light;
For—as I watched the planets—Venus,
    Mars,
Appeared to wax and wane from month to
    month
As though they moved, now near, now far,
    from earth.

Earth could not be their centre. Was the
    sun
Their sovran lord then, as Pythagoras held?
Was this great earth, so 'stablished, so
    secure,
A planet also? Did it also move
Around the sun? If this were true, my
    friends,
No revolution in this world's affairs,
Not that blind maelstrom where imperial
    Rome
Went down into the dark, could so engulf
All that we thought we knew. We who
    believed
In our own majesty, we who walked with
    gods
As younger sons on this proud central stage,
Round which the whole bright firmament
    revolved
For our especial glory, must we creep
Like ants upon our midget ball of dust
Lost in immensity?
                I could not take

That darkness lightly. I withheld my
    book
For many a year, until I clearly saw,
And Rome approved me—have they not
    brought it yet?—
That this tremendous music could not
    drown
The still supernal music of the soul,
Or quench the light that shone when Christ
    was born.
For who, if one lost star could lead the
    kings
To God's own Son, would shrink from
    following these
To His eternal throne?
                  This at the least
We know, the soul of man can soar through
    heaven.
It is our own wild wings that dwarf the
    world
To nothingness beneath us. Let the soul
Take courage, then. If its own thought be
    true,

Not all the immensities of little minds
Can ever quench its own celestial fire.

No. This new night was needed, that the
    soul
Might conquer its own kingdom and arise
To its full stature. So, in face of death,
I saw that I must speak the truth I knew.

Have they not brought it? What delays
    my book?
I am afraid. Tell me the truth, my friends.
At this last hour, the Church may yet
    withhold
Her sanction. Not the Church, but those
    who think
A little darkness helps her.
                              Were this true,
They would do well. If the poor light we
    win
Confuse or blind us, to the Light of lights,
Let all our wisdom perish. I affirm

[30]

A greater Darkness, where the one true
    Church
Shall after all her agonies of loss
And many an age of doubt, perhaps, to
    come,
See this processional host of splendours
    burn
Like tapers round her altar.

                      So I speak
Not for myself, but for the age unborn.
I caught the fire from those who went be-
    fore,
The bearers of the torch who could not see
The goal to which they strained.   I caught
    their fire,
And carried it, only a little way beyond;
But there are those that wait for it, I know,
Those who will carry it on to victory.
I dare not fail them.   Looking back, I see
Those others,—fallen, with their arms out-
    stretched
Dead, pointing to the future.

THE TORCH-BEARERS

                    Far, far back,
Before the Egyptians built their pyramids
With those dark funnels pointing to the
      north,
Through which the Pharaohs from their
      desert tombs
Gaze all night long upon the Polar Star,
Some wandering Arab crept from death to
      life
Led by the Plough across those wastes of
      pearl. . . .

Long, long ago—have they not brought it
      yet?
My book?—I finished it one summer's
      night,
And felt my blood all beating into song.
I meant to print those verses in my book,
A prelude, hinting at that deeper night
Which darkens all our knowledge.   Then
      I thought
The measure moved too lightly.
                    Do you recall

Those verses, Elsa? They would pass the
   time.
How happy I was the night I wrote that
   song!"

Then, one of those bowed shadows raised
   her head
And, like a mother crooning to her child,
Murmured the words he wrote, so long ago.

In old Cathay, in far Cathay,
   Before the western world began,
They saw the moving fount of day
   Eclipsed, as by a shadowy fan;
They stood upon their Chinese wall.
   They saw his fire to ashes fade,
And felt the deeper slumber fall
   On domes of pearl and towers of jade.

With slim brown hands, in Araby,
   They traced, upon the desert sand,
Their Rams and Scorpions of the sky,
   And strove—and failed—to understand.

THE TORCH-BEARERS

Before their footprints were effaced
    The shifting sand forgot their rune;
Their hieroglyphs were all erased,
    Their desert naked to the moon.

In Bagdad of the purple nights,
    Haroun Al Raschid built a tower,
Where sages watched a thousand lights
    And read their legends, for an hour.
The tower is down, the Caliph dead,
    Their astrolabes are wrecked with rust.
Orion glitters overhead,
    Aladdin's lamp is in the dust.

In Babylon, in Babylon,
    They baked their tablets of the clay;
And, year by year, inscribed thereon
    The dark eclipses of their day;
They saw the moving finger write
    Its *Mene, Mene,* on their sun.
A mightier shadow cloaks their light,
    And clay is clay in Babylon.

A shadow moved towards him from the
    door.
Copernicus, with a cry, upraised his head.
"The book, I cannot see it, let me feel
The lettering on the cover.

                      It is here!
Put out the lamp, now. Draw those cur-
    tains back,
And let me die with starlight on my face.
An angel's hand in mine . . . yes; I can
    say
My *nunc dimittis* now . . . light, and more
    light
In that pure realm whose darkness is our
    peace."

II

TYCHO BRAHE

I

THEY thought him a magician, Tycho
    Brahe,
Who lived on that strange island in the
    Sound,
Nine miles from Elsinore.
              His legend reached
The Mermaid Inn the year that Shake-
    speare died.
Fynes Moryson had brought his travellers'
    tales
Of Wheen, the heart-shaped isle where
    Tycho made
His great discoveries, and, with Jeppe, his
    dwarf,

And flaxen-haired Christine, the peasant
girl,
Dreamed his great dreams for five-and-
twenty years.
For there he lit that lanthorn of the
law,
Uraniborg; that fortress of the truth,
With Pegasus flying above its loftiest
tower,
While, in its roofs, like wide enchanted
eyes
Watching, the brightest windows in the
world,
Opened upon the stars.

Nine miles from Elsinore, with all those
ghosts,
There's magic enough in that! But white-
cliffed Wheen,
Six miles in girth, with crowds of hunch-
back waves
Crawling all round it, and those moon-
struck windows,

Held its own magic, too; for Tycho Brahe
By his mysterious alchemy of dreams
Had so enriched the soil, that when the
    king
Of England wished to buy it, Denmark
    asked
'A price too great for any king on earth.
"Give us," they said, "in scarlet cardinal's
    cloth
Enough to cover it, and, at every corner,
Of every piece, a right rose-noble too;
Then all that kings can buy of Wheen is
    yours.
Only," said they, "a merchant bought it
    once;
And, when he came to claim it, goblins
    flocked
All round him, from its forty goblin
    farms,
And mocked him, bidding him take away
    the stones
That he had bought, for nothing else was
    his."

These things were fables.   They were also
    true.
They thought him a magician, Tycho Brahe,
The astrologer, who wore the mask of gold.
Perhaps he was.   There's magic in the
    truth;
And only those who find and follow its laws
Can work its miracles.

                Tycho sought the truth
From that strange year in boyhood when he
    heard
The great eclipse foretold; and, on the day
Appointed, at the very minute even,
Beheld the weirdly punctual shadow creep
Across the sun, bewildering all the birds
With thoughts of evening.

                Picture him, on that day,
The boy at Copenhagen, with his mane
Of thick red hair, thrusting his freckled
    face
Out of his upper window, holding the piece
Of glass he blackened above his candle-
    flame

To watch that orange ember in the sky
Wane into smouldering ash.
           He whispered there,
"So it is true. By searching in the heavens,
Men can foretell the future."
                In the street
Below him, throngs were babbling of the
    plague
That might or might not follow.
                He resolved
To make himself the master of that deep
    art
And know what might be known.
             He bought the books
Of Stadius, with his tables of the stars.
Night after night, among the gabled roofs,
Climbing and creeping through a world
    unknown
Save to the roosting stork, he learned to
    find
The constellations, Cassiopeia's throne,
The Plough still pointing to the Polar Star,
The sword-belt of Orion. There he watched

The movements of the planets, hours on
    hours,
And wondered at the mystery of it all.

All this he did in secret, for his birth
Was noble, and such wonderings were a
    sign
Of low estate, when Tycho Brahe was
    young;
And all his kinsmen hoped that Tycho
    Brahe
Would live, serene as they, among his dogs
And horses; or, if honour must be won,
Let the superfluous glory flow from fields
Where blood might still be shed; or from
    those courts
Where statesmen lie. But Tycho sought
    the truth.
So, when they sent him in his tutor's charge
To Leipzig, for such studies as they held
More worthy of his princely blood, he
    searched
The Almagest; and, while his tutor slept,
Measured the delicate angles of the stars,

THE TORCH-BEARERS

Out of his window, with his compasses,
His only instrument.   Even with this rude
    aid
He found so many an ancient record wrong
That more and more he burned to find the
    truth.

One night at home, as Tycho searched the
    sky,
Out of his window, compasses in hand,
Fixing one point upon a planet, one
Upon some loftier star, a ripple of laughter
Startled him, from the garden walk below.
He lowered his compass, peered into the
    dark
And saw—Christine, the blue-eyed peasant
    girl,
With bare brown feet, standing among the
    flowers.

She held what seemed an apple in her
    hand;
And, in a voice that Aprilled all his blood,

The low soft voice of earth, drawing him
    down
From those cold heights to that warm breast
    of Spring,
A natural voice that had not learned to
    use
The false tones of the world, simple and
    clear
As a bird's voice, out of the fragrant dark-
    ness called,
"I saw it falling from your window-ledge!
I thought it was an apple, till it rolled
Over my foot.

               It's heavy.   Shall I try
To throw it back to you?"

                  Tycho saw a stain
Of purple across one small arched glisten-
    ing foot.
"Your foot is bruised," he cried.

                  "O no," she laughed,
And plucked the stain off. "Only a petal,
    see."
She showed it to him.

"But this—I wonder now
If I can throw it."
        Twice she tried and failed;
Or Tycho failed to catch that slippery
    sphere.
He saw the supple body swaying below,
The ripe red lips that parted as she laughed,
And those deep eyes where all the stars
    were drowned.

At the third time he caught it; and she
    vanished,
Waving her hand, a little floating moth,
Between the pine-trees, into the warm dark
    night.
He turned into his room, and quickly thrust
Under his pillow that forbidden fruit;
For the door opened, and the hot red face
Of Otto Brahe, his father, glowered at him.
"What's this?   What's this?"
        The furious-eyed old man
Limped to the bedside, pulled the mystery
    out,

And stared upon the strangest apple of Eve
That ever troubled Eden,—heavy as bronze,
And delicately enchased with silver stars,
The small celestial globe that Tycho bought
In Leipzig.

      Then the storm burst on his head!
This moon - struck 'pothecary's - prentice
    work,
These cheap-jack calendar-maker's gypsy
    tricks
Would damn the mother of any Knutsdorp
    squire,
And crown his father like a stag of ten.
Quarrel on quarrel followed from that
    night,
Till Tycho sickened of his ancient name;
And, wandering through the woods about
    his home,
Found on a hill-top, ringed with fragrant
    pines,
A little open glade of whispering ferns.
Thither, at night, he stole to watch the stars;
And there he told the oldest tale on earth

To one that watched beside him, one whose
    eyes
Shone with true love, more beautiful than
    the stars,
A daughter of earth, the peasant-girl,
    Christine.

They met there, in the dusk, on his last
    night
At home, before he went to Wittenberg.
They stood knee-deep among the whisper-
    ing ferns,
And said good-bye.
              "I shall return," he said,
"And shame them for their folly, who
    would set
Their pride above the stars, Christine, and
    you.
At Wittenberg or Rostoch I shall find
More chances and more knowledge. All
    those worlds
Are still to conquer. We know nothing
    yet;

The books are crammed with fables. They
    foretell
Here an eclipse, and there a dawning moon,
But most of them were out a month or more
On Jupiter and Saturn.

                    There's one way,
And only one, to knowledge of the law
Whereby the stars are steered, and so to read
The future, even perhaps the destinies
Of men and nations,—only one sure way,
And that's to watch them, watch them, and
    record
The truth we know, and not the lies we
    dream.
Dear, while I watch them, though the hills
    and sea
Divide us, every night our eyes can meet
Among those constant glories. Every night
Your eyes and mine, upraised to that bright
    realm,
Can, in one moment, speak across the world.
I shall come back with knowledge and with
    power,

And you—will wait for me?"
                    She answered him
In silence, with the starlight of her eyes.

II

He watched the skies at Wittenberg.   The
    plague
Drove him to Rostoch, and he watched
    them there;
But, even there, the plague of little
    minds
Beset him.   At a wedding-feast he met
His noble countryman, Manderup, who
    asked,
With mocking courtesy, whether Tycho
    Brahe
Was ready yet to practise his black art
At country fairs.   The guests, and Tycho,
    laughed;
Whereat the swaggering Junker blandly
    sneered,
"If fortune-telling fail, Christine will
    dance,

[48]

Thus—tambourine on hip," he struck a
  pose.
"Her pretty feet will pack that booth of
  yours."
They fought, at midnight, in a wood, with
  swords.
And not a spark of light but those that leapt
Blue from the clashing blades. Tycho had
  lost
His moon and stars awhile, almost his life;
For, in one furious bout, his enemy's blade
Dashed like a scribble of lightning into the
  face
Of Tycho Brahe, and left him spluttering
  blood,
Groping through that dark wood with out-
  stretched hands,
To fall in a death-black swoon.
                      They carried him back
To Rostoch; and when Tycho saw at last
That mirrored patch of mutilated flesh,
Seared as by fire, between the frank blue
  eyes

[49]

And firm young mouth where, like a living
    flower
Upon some stricken tree, youth lingered
    still,
He'd but one thought, Christine would
    shrink from him
In fear, or worse, in pity. An end had
    come
Worse than old age, to all the glory of
    youth.
Urania would not let her lover stray
Into a mortal's arms. He must remain
Her own, for ever; and for ever, alone.

Yet, as the days went by, to face the world,
He made himself a delicate mask of gold
And silver, shaped like those that minstrels
    wear
At carnival in Venice, or when love,
Disguising its disguise of mortal flesh,
Wooes as a nameless prince from far away.
And when this world's day, with its blaze
    and coil

Was ended, and the first white star awoke
In that pure realm where all our tumults
    die,
His eyes and hers, meeting on Hesperus,
Renewed their troth.
             He seemed to see Christine,
Ringed by the pine-trees on that distant hill,
A small white figure, lost in space and time,
Yet gazing at the sky, and conquering all,
Height, depth, and heaven itself, by the
    sheer power
Of love at one with everlasting laws,
A love that shared the constancy of heaven,
And spoke to him across, above, the world.

III

Not till he crossed the Danube did he find
Among the fountains and the storied eaves
Of Augsburg, one to share his task with
    him.
Paul Hainzel, of that city, greatly loved
To talk with Tycho of the strange new
    dreams

[51]

Copernicus had kindled. Did this earth
Move? Was the sun the centre of our
  scheme?
And Tycho told him, there is but one way
To know the truth, and that's to sweep
  aside
All the dark cobwebs of old sophistry,
And watch and learn that moving alphabet,
Each smallest silver character inscribed
Upon the skies themselves, noting them
  down,
Till on a day we find them taking shape
In phrases, with a meaning; and, at last,
The hard-won beauty of that celestial book
With all its epic harmonies unfold
Like some great poet's universal song.

He was a great magician, Tycho Brahe.
"Hainzel," he said, "we have no magic
  wand,
But what the truth can give us. If we find
Even with a compass, through a bedroom
  window,

[52]

That half the glittering Almagest is wrong,
Think you, what noble conquests might be
    ours,
Had we but nobler instruments."

                                    He showed
Quivering with eagerness, his first rude
    plan
For that great quadrant,—not the wooden
    toy
Of old Scultetus, but a kingly weapon,
Huge as a Roman battering-ram, and fine
In its divisions as any goldsmith's work.
"It could be built," said Tycho, "but the
    cost
Would buy a dozen culverin for your
    wars."
Then Hainzel, fired by Tycho's burning
    brain,
Answered, "We'll make it. We've a war,
    to wage
On Chaos, and his kingdoms of the night."
They chose the cunningest artists of the
    town,

[53]

THE TORCH-BEARERS

Clock-makers, jewellers, carpenters, and
    smiths,
And, setting them all afire with Tycho's
    dream,
Within a month his dream was oak and
    brass.
Its beams were fourteen cubits, solid oak,
Banded with iron. Its arch was polished
    brass
Whereon five thousand exquisite divisions
Were marked to show the minutes of
    degrees.

So huge and heavy it was, a score of
    men,
Could hardly drag and fix it to its place
In Hainzel's garden.
            Many a shining night,
Tycho and Hainzel, out of that maze of
    flowers,
Charted the stars, discovering point by
    point,

How all the records erred, until the fame
Of this new master, hovering above the
    schools
Like a strange hawk, threatened the creep-
    ing dreams
Of all the Aristotelians, and began
To set their mouse-holes twittering "Tycho
    Brahe!"

Then Tycho Brahe came home, to find
    Christine.
Up to that whispering glade of ferns he
    sped,
At the first wink of Hesperus.

                      He stood
In shadow, under the darkest pine, to hide
The little golden mask upon his face.
He wondered, will she shrink from me in
    fear
Or loathing? Will she even come at all?
And, as he wondered, like a light she moved
Before him.

"Is it you?"—
            "Christine! Christine,"
He whispered, "It is I, the mountebank,
Playing a jest upon you. It's only a mask!
Do not be frightened. I am here behind
    it."

Her red lips parted, and between them
    shone,
The little teeth like white pomegranate
    seeds.
He saw her frightened eyes.
                    Then, with a cry,
Her arms went round him, and her eyelids
    closed.
Lying against his heart, she set her lips
Against his lips, and claimed him for her
    own.

IV

One frosty night, as Tycho bent his way
Home to the dark old abbey, he upraised
His eyes, and saw a portent in the sky.

There, in its most familiar patch of blue,
Where Cassiopeia's five-fold glory burned,
An unknown brilliance quivered, a huge
    star
Unseen before, a strange new visitant
To heavens unchangeable, as the world be-
    lieved,
Since the creation.
                  Could new stars be born?
Night after night he watched that miracle
Growing and changing colour as it grew;
White at the first, and large as Jupiter;
And, in the third month, yellow, and larger
    yet;
Red in the fifth month, like Aldebaran,
And larger even than Lyra.   In the seventh,
Bluish like Saturn; whence it dulled and
    dwined
Little by little, till after eight months more
Into the dark abysmal blue of night,
Whence it arose, the wonder died away.
But, while it blazed above him, Tycho
    brought

THE TORCH-BEARERS

Those delicate records of two hundred
    nights
To Copenhagen. There, in his golden
    mask,
At supper with Pratensis, who believed
Only what old books told him, Tycho met
Dancey, the French Ambassador, rainbow-
    gay
In satin hose and doublet, supple and thin,
Brown-eyed, and bearded with a soft black
    tuft
Neat as a blackbird's wing,—a spirit as
    keen
And swift as France on all the starry trails
Of thought.
        He saw the deep and simple fire,
The mystery of all genius in those eyes
Above that golden vizard.
              Tycho raised
His wine-cup, brimming—they thought—
    with purple dreams;
And bade them drink to their triumphant
    Queen

[58]

Of all the Muses, to their Lady of Light
Urania, and the great new star.

                        They laughed,
Thinking the young astrologer's golden
    mask
Hid a sardonic jest.

                "The skies are clear,"
Said Tycho Brahe, "and we have eyes to
    see.
Put out your candles.   Open those windows
    there!"
The colder darkness breathed upon their
    brows,
And Tycho pointed, into the deep blue
    night.
There, in their most immutable height of
    heaven,
In *ipso cælo,* in the ethereal realm,
Beyond all planets, red as Mars it burned,
The one impossible glory.

                  "But it's true!"
Pratensis gasped; then, clutching the first
    straw,

"Now I recall how Pliny the Elder said,
Hipparchus also saw a strange new star,
Not where the comets, not where the *Rosæ*
    bloom
And fade, but in that solid crystal sphere
Where nothing changes."
              Tycho smiled, and showed
The record of his watchings.
                   "But the world
Must know all this," cried Dancey. "You
    must print it."
"Print it?" said Tycho, turning that golden
    mask
On both his friends. "Could I, a noble,
    print
This trafficking with Urania in a book?
They'd hound me out of Denmark! This
    disgrace
Of work, with hands or brain, no matter
    why,
No matter how, in one who ought to
    dwell

Fixed to the solid upper sphere, my friends,
Would never be forgiven."

　　　　　　　　Dancey stared
In mute amazement, but that mask of gold
Outstared him, sphinx-like, and inscrutable.

Soon through all Europe, like the blinded
　　　moths,
Roused by a lantern in old palaces
Among the mouldering tapestries of
　　　thought,
Weird fables woke and fluttered to and fro,
And wild-eyed sages hunted them for truth.
The Italian, Frangipani, thought the star
The lost Electra, that had left her throne
Among the Pleiads, and plunged into the
　　　night
Like a veiled mourner, when Troy town
　　　was burned.
The German painter, Busch, of Erfurt,
　　　wrote,
"It was a comet, made of mortal sins;

A poisonous mist, touched by the wrath of
    God
To fire; from which there would descend
    on earth
All manner of evil—plagues and sudden
    death,
Frenchmen and famine."
              Preachers thumped and raved.
Theodore Beza in Calvin's pulpit tore
His grim black gown, and vowed it was the
    Star
That led the Magi. It had now returned
To mark the world's end and the Judgment
    Day.
Then, in this hubbub, Dancey told the king
Of Denmark, "There is one who knows the
    truth—
Your subject Tycho Brahe, who, night by
    night,
Watched and recorded all that truth could
    see.
It would bring honour to all Denmark, sire,
If Tycho could forget his rank awhile,

And print these great discoveries in a book,
For all the world to read."
           So Tycho Brahe
Received a letter in the king's own hand,
Urging him, "Truth is the one pure foun-
    tain-head
Of all nobility. Pray forget your rank."
His noble kinsmen echoed, "If you wish
To please His Majesty and ourselves, forget
Your rank."
          "I will," said Tycho Brahe;
"Your reasoning has convinced me. I will
    print
My book, *De Nova Stella.'* And to prove
All you have said concerning temporal
    rank
And this eternal truth you love so well,
I marry, to-day,"—they foamed, but all
    their mouths
Were stopped and stuffed and sealed with
    their own words,—
"I marry to-day my own true love, Chris-
    tine."

[63]

V

They thought him a magician, Tycho
    Brahe.
Perhaps he was.   There's magic all around
    us
In rocks and trees, and in the minds of men,
Deep hidden springs of magic.

                     He that strikes
The rock aright, may find them where he
    will.

And Tycho tasted happiness in his hour.
There was a prince in Denmark in those
    days;
And, when he heard how other kings
    desired
The secrets of this new astrology,
He said, "This man, in after years, will
    bring
Glory to Denmark, honour to her prince.
He is a Dane. Give him this isle of
    Wheen,

[64]

And let him make his great discoveries
    there.
Let him have gold to buy his instruments,
And build his house and his observatory."

So Tycho set this island where he lived
Whispering with wizardry; and, in its
    heart,
He lighted that strange lanthorn of the law,
And built himself that wonder of the world,
Uraniborg, a fortress for the truth,
A city of the heavens.

               Around it ran
A mighty rampart twenty-two feet high,
And twenty feet in thickness at the base.
Its angles pointed north, south, east and
    west,
With gates and turrets; and, within this wall,
Were fruitful orchards, apple, and cherry,
    and pear;
And, sheltered in their midst from all but
    sun,
A garden, warm and busy with singing bees.

THE TORCH-BEARERS

There, many an hour, his flaxen-haired
    Christine,
Sang to her child, her first-born, Magdalen,
Or watched her playing, a flower among the
    flowers.
Dark in the centre of that zone of bliss
Arose the magic towers of Tycho Brahe.
Two of them had great windows in their
    roofs
Opening upon the sky where'er he willed,
And under these observatories he made
A library of many a golden book;
Poets and sages of old Greece and Rome,
And many a mellow legend, many a dream
Of dawning truth in Egypt, or the dusk
Of Araby.   Under all of these he made
A subterranean crypt for alchemy,
With sixteen furnaces; and, under this,
He sank a well, so deep, that Jeppe declared
He had tapped the central fountains of the
    world,
And drew his magic from those cold clear
    springs.

This was the very well, said Jeppe, the
    dwarf,
Where Truth was hidden; but, by Tycho
    Brahe
And his weird skill, the magic water flowed,
Through pipes, uphill, to all the house
    above:
The kitchen where his cooks could broil a
    trout
For sages or prepare a feast for kings;
The garrets for the students in the roof;
The guest-rooms, and the red room to the
    north,
The study and the blue room to the south;
The small octagonal yellow room that held
The sunlight like a jewel all day long,
And Magdalen, with her happy dreams, at
    night;
Then, facing to the west, one long green
    room,
The ceiling painted like the bower of Eve
With flowers and leaves, the windows open-
    ing wide

THE TORCH-BEARERS

Through which Christine and Tycho Brahe
    at dawn
Could see the white sails drifting on the
    Sound
Like petals from their orchard.
                       To the north,
He built a printing house for noble books,
Poems, and those deep legends of the sky,
Still to be born at his Uraniborg.
Beyond the rampart to the north arose
A workshop for his instruments. To the
    south
A low thatched farm-house rambled round
    a yard
Alive with clucking hens; and, further yet
To southward on another hill, he made
A great house for his larger instruments,
And called it Stiernborg, mountain of the
    stars.

And, on his towers and turrets, Tycho set
Statues with golden verses in the praise

WATCHERS OF THE SKY

Of famous men, the bearers of the torch,
From Ptolemy to the new Copernicus.
Then, in that storm-proof mountain of the
    stars,
He set in all their splendour of new-made
    brass
His armouries for the assault of heaven,—
Circles in azimuth, armillary spheres,
Revolving zodiacs with great brazen rings;
Quadrants of solid brass, ten cubits broad,
Brass parallactic rules, made to revolve
In azimuth; clocks with wheels; an astro-
    labe;
And that large globe strengthened by oaken
    beams
He made at Augsburg.
              All his gold he spent;
But Denmark had a prince in those great
    days;
And, in his brain, the dreams of Tycho
    Brahe
Kindled a thirst for glory. So he made

THE TORCH-BEARERS

Tycho the Lord of sundry lands and rents,
And Keeper of the Chapel where the kings
Of Oldenburg were buried; for he said
"To whom could all these kings entrust
    their bones
More fitly than to him who read the stars,
And though a mortal, knew immortal laws;
And paced, at night, the silent halls of
    heaven."

VI

He was a great magician, Tycho Brahe.
There, on his island, for a score of years,
He watched the skies, recording star on
    star,
For future ages, and, by patient toil,
Perfected his great tables of the sun,
The moon, the planets.
                      There, too happy far
For any history, sons and daughters rose,
A little clan of love, around Christine;
And Tycho thought, when I am dead, my
    sons

Will rule and work in my Uraniborg.
And yet a doubt would trouble him, for he
    knew
The children of Christine would still be
    held
Ignoble, by the world.
                  Disciples came,
Young-eyed and swift, the bearers of the
    torch
From many a city to Uraniborg,
And Tycho Brahe received them like a
    king,
And bade them light their torches at his
    fire.
The King of Scotland came, with all his
    court,
And dwelt eight days in Tycho Brahe's
    domain,
Asking him many a riddle, deep and dark,
Whose answer, none the less, a king should
    know.
What boots it on this earth to be a king,
To rule a part of earth, and not to know

The worth of his own realm, whether he
    rule
As God's vice-gerent, and his realm be still
The centre of the centre of all worlds;
Or whether, as Copernicus proclaimed,
This earth itself be moving, a lost grain
Of dust among the innumerable stars?
For this would dwarf all glory but the soul,
In king or peasant, that can hail the truth,
Though truth should slay it.

                So to Tycho Brahe,
The king became a subject for eight days.
But, in the crowded hall, when he had gone,
Jeppe raised his matted head, with a
    chuckle of glee,
Quiet as the gurgle of joy in a dark rock-
    pool,
When the first ripple and wash of the first
    spring-tide
Flows bubbling under the dry sun-black-
    ened fringe
Of seaweed, setting it all afloat again,
In magical colours, like a merman's hair.

"Jeppe has a thought," the gay young stu-
    dents cried,
Thronging him round, for all believed that
    Jeppe
Was fey, and had strange visions of the
    truth.
"What is the thought, Jeppe?"
                "I can think no thoughts,"
Croaked Jeppe. "But I have made myself
    a song."
"Silence," they cried, "for Jeppe the night-
    ingale!
Sing, Jeppe!"
  And, wagging his great head to and fro
Before the fire, with deep dark eyes, he
    crooned:

THE SONG OF JEPPE

"What!" said the king,
    "Is earth a bird or bee?
Can this uncharted boundless realm of
    ours

Drone thro' the sky, with leagues of strug-
    gling sea,
  Forests, and hills, and towns, and palace-
    towers?"
"Ay," said the dwarf,
    "I have watched from Stiernborg's
    crown
  Her far dark rim uplift against the
    sky;
But, while earth soars, men say the stars
    go down;
  And, while earth sails, men say the stars
    go by."
An elvish tale!
    Ask Jeppe, the dwarf! *He* knows.
  That's why his eyes look fey; for, chuck-
    ling deep,
Heels over head amongst the stars he goes,
  As all men go; but most are sound asleep.
King, saint, sage,
    Even those that count it true,
  Act as this miracle touched them not at
    all.

They are borne, undizzied, thro' the rush-
    ing blue,
  And build their empires on a sky-tossed
    ball.

Then said the king,
    "If earth so lightly move,
  What of my realm? O, what shall now
    stand sure?"
"Naught," said the dwarf, "in all this
    world, but love.
  All else is dream-stuff and shall not en-
    dure.
'Tis nearer now!
    Our universe hath no centre,
  Our shadowy earth and fleeting heavens
    no stay,
But that deep inward realm which each
    can enter,
  Even Jeppe, the dwarf, by his own secret
    way."

"Where?" said the king,

"O, where? I have not found it!"
"Here," said the dwarf, and music echoed
    "here."
"This infinite circle hath no line to bound
    it;
Therefore that deep strange centre is
    everywhere.
Let the earth soar thro' heaven, that centre
    abideth;
Or plunge to the pit, His covenant still
    holds true.
In the heart of a dying bird, the Master
    hideth;
In the soul of a king," said the dwarf,
    "and in *my* soul, too."

VII

Princes and courtiers came, a few to seek
A little knowledge, many more to gape
In wonder at Tycho's gold and silver mask;
Or when they saw the beauty of his towers,
Envy and hate him for them.

WATCHERS OF THE SKY

Thus arose

The small grey cloud upon the distant sky,
That broke in storm at last.

"Beware," croaked Jeppe,

Lifting his shaggy head beside the fire,
When guests like these had gone, "Master,
    beware!"
And Tycho of the frank blue eyes would
    laugh.
Even when he found Witichius playing
    him false
  His anger, like a momentary breeze,
Died on the dreaming deep; for Tycho
    Brahe
Turned to a nobler riddle,—"Have you
    thought,"
He asked his young disciples, "how the sea
Is moved to that strange rhythm we call
    the tides?
He that can answer this shall have his
    name
Honoured among the bearers of the torch
While Pegasus flies above Uraniborg.

[77].

THE TORCH-BEARERS

I was delayed three hours or more to-day
By the neap-tide. The fishermen on the
    coast
Are never wrong. They time it by the moon.
Post hoc, perhaps, not *propter hoc;* and yet
Through all the changes of the sky and sea
That old white clock of ours with the bat-
    tered face
Does seem infallible.

               There's a love-song too,
The sailors on the coast of Sweden sing,
I have often pondered it. Your courtly
    poets
Upbraid the inconstant moon. ·But these
    men know
The moon and sea are lovers, and they move
In a most constant measure. Hear the
    words
And tell me, if you can, what silver chains
Bind them together." Then, in a voice as
    low
And rhythmical as the sea, he spoke that
    song:

[78]

WATCHERS OF THE SKY

THE SHEPHERDESS OF THE SEA

Reproach not yet our sails' delay;
You cannot see the shoaling bay,
The banks of sand, the fretful bars,
That ebb left naked to the stars.
   The sea's white shepherdess, the moon,
   Shall lead us into harbour soon.

Dear, when you see her glory shine
Between your fragrant boughs of pine,
Know there is but one hour to wait
Before her hands unlock the gate,
   And the full flood of singing foam
   Follow her lovely footsteps home.

Then waves like flocks of silver sheep
Come rustling inland from the deep,
And into rambling valleys press
Behind their heavenly shepherdess.
   You cannot see them? Lift your eyes
   And see their mistress in the skies.
She rises with her silver bow.

[79]

I feel the tide begin to flow;
And every thought and hope and dream
Follow her call, and homeward stream.
Borne on the universal tide,
The wanderer hastens to his bride.
 The sea's white shepherdess, the moon,
Shall lead him into harbour, soon.

VIII

He was a great magician, Tycho Brahe,
But not so great that he could read the
 heart
Or rule the hand of princes.
     When his friend
King Frederick died, the young Prince
 Christian reigned;
And, round him, fool and knave made com-
 mon cause
Against the magic that could pour their
 gold
Into a gulf of stars. This Tycho Brahe
Had grown too proud. He held them in
 contempt,

So they believed; for, when he spoke, their
    thoughts
Crept at his feet like spaniels. Junkerdom
Felt it was foolish, for he towered above it,
And so it hated him. Did he not spend
Gold that a fool could spend as quickly
    as he?
Were there not great estates bestowed upon
    him
In wisdom's name, that from the dawn of
    time
Had been the natural right of Junkerdom?
And would he not bequeath them to his
    heirs,
The children of Christine, an unfree
    woman?
"Why you, sire, even you," they told the
    king,
"He has made a laughing-stock. That horo-
    scope
He read for you, the night when you were
    born,
Printed, and bound it in green velvet, too,—

[81]

Read it. The whole world laughs at it.
    He said
That Venus was the star that ruled your
    fate,
And Venus would destroy you. Tycho
    Brahe
Inspired your royal father with the fear
That kept your youth so long in leading-
    strings,
The fear that every pretty hedgerow flower
Would be your Circe. So he thought to
    avenge
Our mockery of this peasant-girl Chris-
    tine,
To whom, indeed, he plays the faithful
    swine,
Knowing full well his gold and silver nose
Would never win another."
                    Thus the sky
Darkened above Uraniborg, and those
Who dwelt within it, till one evil day,
One seeming happy day, when Tycho
    marked

The seven-hundredth star upon his chart,
Two pompous officers from Walchendorp,
The chancellor, knocked at Tycho's eastern
    gate.
"We are sent," they said, "to see and to
    report
What use you make of these estates of
    yours.
Your alchemy has turned more gold to lead
Than Denmark can approve. The uses
    now!
Show us the uses of this work of yours."
Then Tycho showed his tables of the stars,
Seven hundred stars, each noted in its place
With exquisite precision, the result
Of watching heaven for five-and-twenty
    years.
"And is this all?" they said.
                They sought to invent
Some ground for damning him. The truth
    alone
Would serve them, as it seemed. For these
    were men

Who could not understand.

      "Not all, I hope,"
Said Tycho, "for I think, before I die,
I shall have marked a thousand."

        "To what end?
When shall we reap the fruits of all this
  toil?
Show us its uses."

       "In the time to come,"
Said Tycho Brahe, "perhaps a hundred
  years,
Perhaps a thousand, when our own poor
  names
Are quite forgotten, and our kingdoms dust,
On one sure certain day, the torch-bearers
Will, at some point of contact, see a light
Moving upon this chaos. Though our eyes
Be shut for ever in an iron sleep,
Their eyes shall see the kingdom of the
  law,
Our undiscovered cosmos. They shall see
  it,—
A new creation rising from the deep,

[84]

Beautiful, whole.

     We are like men that hear
Disjointed notes of some supernal choir.
Year after year, we patiently record
All we can gather. In that far-off time,
A people that we have not known shall
  hear them,
Moving like music to a single end."

They could not understand: this life that
  sought
Only to bear the torch and hand it on;
And so they made report that all the dreams
Of Tycho Brahe were fruitless; perilous,
  too,
Since he avowed that any fruit they bore
Would fall, in distant years, to alien hands.

Little by little, Walchendorp withdrew
His rents from Tycho Brahe, accusing him
Of gross neglects. The Chapel at Ros-
  kilde
Was falling into ruin. Tycho Brahe

Was Keeper of the Bones of Oldenburg.
He must rebuild the Chapel. All the gifts
That Frederick gave to help him in his
    task,
Were turned to stumbling-blocks; till, one
    dark day,
He called his young disciples round him
    there,
And in that mellow library of dreams,
Lit by the dying sunset, poured his heart
And mind before them, bidding them fare-
    well.
Through the wide-open windows as he
    spoke
They heard the sorrowful whisper of the
    sea
Ebbing and flowing around Uraniborg.
"An end has come," he said, "to all we
    planned.
Uraniborg has drained her treasury dry.
Your Alma Mater now must close her gates
On you, her guests; on me; and, worst of
    all,

WATCHERS OF THE SKY

On one most dear, who made this place my
    home.
For you are young, your homes are all to
    win,
And you would all have gone your sepa-
    rate ways
In a brief while; and, though I think you
    love
Your college of the skies, it could not
    mean
All that it meant to those who called it
    'home.'

You that have worked with me, for one
    brief year,
Will never quite forget Uraniborg.
This room, the sunset gilding all those
    books,
The star-charts, and that old celestial globe,
The long bright evenings by the winter fire,
Of Tycho Brahe were fruitless; perilous
The talk that opened heaven, the songs
    you sung,

Yes, even, I think, the tricks you played
   with Jeppe,
Will somehow, when yourselves are grow-
   ing old,
Be hallowed into beauty, touched with
   tears,
For you will wish they might be yours
   again.

These have been mine for five-and-twenty
   years,
And more than these,—the work, the
   dreams I shared
With you, and others here.   My heart will
   break
To leave them.   But the appointed time has
   come
As it must come to all men.
                              You and I
Have watched too many constant stars to
   dream
That heaven or earth, the destinies of men

Or nations, are the sport of chance. An
   end
Comes to us all through blindness, age, or
   death.
If mine must come in exile, it shall find me
Bearing the torch as far as I can bear it,
Until I fall at the feet of the young run-
   ner,
Who takes it from me, and carries it out
   of sight,
Into the great new age I shall not know,
Into the great new realms I must not tread.
Come, then, swift-footed, let me see you
   stand
Waiting before me, crowned with youth and
   joy,
At the next turning. Take it from my hand,
For I am almost ready now to fall.

Something I have achieved, yes, though I
   say it,
I have not loitered on that fiery way.

THE TORCH-BEARERS

And if I front the judgment of the wise
In centuries to come, with more of dread
Than my destroyers, it is because this work
Will be of use, remembered and appraised,
When all their hate is dead.

                    I say the work,
Not the blind rumour, the glory or fame of
    it.
These observations of seven hundred stars
Are little enough in sight of those great
    hosts
Which nightly wheel around us, though I
    hope,
Yes, I still hope, in some more generous
    land
To make my thousand up before I die.
Little enough, I know,—a midget's work!
The men that follow me, with more delicate
    art
May add their tens of thousands; yet my
    sum
Will save them just that five-and-twenty
    years

Of patience, bring them sooner to their
    goal,
That kingdom of the law I shall not see.
We are on the verge of great discoveries.
I feel them as a dreamer feels the dawn
Before his eyes are opened. Many of you
Will see them. In that day you will recall
This, our last meeting at Uraniborg,
And how I told you that this work of ours
Would lead to victories for the coming age.
The victors may forget us. What of that?
Theirs be the palms, the shouting, and the
    praise.
Ours be the fathers' glory in the sons.
Ours the delight of giving, the deep joy
Of labouring, on the cliff's face, all night
    long,
Cutting them foot-holes in the solid rock,
Whereby they climb so gaily to the heights,
And gaze upon their new-discovered
    worlds.
You will not find me there. When you
    descend,

THE TORCH-BEARERS

Look for me in the darkness at the foot
Of those high cliffs, under the drifted
leaves.

That's where we hide at last, we pioneers,
For we are very proud, and must be sought
Before the world can find us, in our graves.
There have been compensations. I have
seen
In darkness, more perhaps than eyes can see
When sunlight blinds them on the moun-
tain-tops;
Guessed at a glory past our mortal range,
And only mine because the night was mine.

Of those three systems of the universe,
The Ptolemaic, held by all the schools,
May yet be proven false. We yet may find
This earth of ours is not the sovran lord
Of all those wheeling spheres. Ourselves
have marked
Movements among the planets that forbid
Acceptance of it wholly. Some of these
Are moving round the sun, if we can trust

Our years of watching.   There are stranger
    dreams.
This radical, Copernicus, the priest,
Of whom I often talked with you, declares
All of these movements can be reconciled,
If—a hypothesis only—we should take
The sun itself for centre, and assume
That this huge earth, so 'stablished, so se-
    cure
In its foundations, is a planet also,
And moves around the sun.
                  I cannot think it.
This leap of thought is yet too great for
    me.
I have no doubt that Ptolemy was wrong.
Some of his planets move around the sun.
Copernicus is nearer to the truth
In some things.   But the planets we have
    watched
Still wander from the course that he as-
    signed.
Therefore, my system, which includes the
    best

Of both, I hold may yet be proven true.
This earth of ours, as Jeppe declared one
    day,
So simply that we laughed, is 'much too big
To move,' so let it be the centre still,
And let the planets move around their sun;
But let the sun with all its planets move
Around our central earth.

                This at the least
Accords with all we know, and saves man-
    kind
From that enormous plunge into the night;
Saves them from voyaging for ten thousand
    years
Through boundless darkness without sight
    of land;
Saves them from all that agony of loss,
As one by one the beacon-fires of faith
Are drowned in blackness.

            I beseech you, then,
Let me be proven wrong, before you take
That darkness lightly. If at last you find⬤

The proven facts against me, take the
    plunge.
Launch out into that darkness. Let the
    lamps
Of heaven, the glowing hearth-fires that
    we knew
Die out behind you, while the freshening
    wind
Blows on your brows, and overhead you see
The stars of truth that lead you from your
    home.

I love this island,—every little glen,
Hazel-wood, brook, and fish-pond; every
    bough
And blossom in that garden; and I hoped
To die here. But it is not chance, I know,
That sends me wandering through the
    world again.
My use perhaps is ended; and the power
That made me, breaks me."

                  As he spoke, they saw

The tears upon his face. He bowed his
  head
And left them silent in the darkened room.
They saw his face no more.

              The self-same hour,
Tycho, Christine, and all their children,
  left
Their island-home for ever. In their ship
They took a few of the smaller instruments,
And that most precious record of the stars,
His legacy to the future. Into the night
They vanished, leaving on the ghostly cliffs
Only one dark, distorted, dog-like shape
To watch them, sobbing, under its matted
  hair,
"Master, have you forgotten Jeppe, your
  dwarf?"

IX

He was a great magician, Tycho Brahe,
And yet his magic, under changing skies,
Could never change his heart, or touch the
  hills

Of those far countries with the tints of
    home.
And, after many a month of wandering,
He came to Prague; and, though with open
    hands
Rodolphe received him, like an exiled king,
A new Æneas, exiled for the truth
(For so they called him), none could heal
    the wounds
That bled within, or lull his grief to sleep
With that familiar whisper of the waves,
Ebbing and flowing around Uraniborg.

Doggedly still he laboured; point by point,
Crept on, with aching heart and burning
    brain,
Until his table of the stars had reached
The thousand that he hoped, to crown his
    toil.
But Christine heard him murmuring in the
    night,
"The work, the work! Not to have lived
    in vain!

[97]

THE TORCH-BEARERS

Into whose hands can I entrust it all?
I thought to find him standing by the way,
Waiting to seize the splendour from my
    hand,
The swift, young-eyed runner with the
    torch.
Let me not live in vain, let me not fall
Before I yield it to the appointed soul."
And yet the Power that made and broke
    him heard:
For, on a certain day, to Tycho came
Another exile, guided through the dark
Of Europe by the starlight in his eyes,
Or that invisible hand which guides the
    world.
He asked him, as the runner with the torch
Alone could ask, asked as a natural right
For Tycho's hard-won life-work, those re-
    sults,
His tables of the stars.   He gave his name
Almost as one who told him, *It is I;*
And yet unconscious that he told; a name

Not famous yet, though truth had marked
    him out
Already, by his exile, as her own,—
The name of Johann Kepler.
                "It was strange,"
Wrote Kepler, not long after, "for I asked
Unheard-of things, and yet he gave them to
    me
As if I were his son. When first I saw him,
We seemed to have known each other years
    ago
In some forgotten world. I could not guess
That Tycho Brahe was dying. He was
    quick
Of temper, and we quarrelled now and
    then,
Only to find ourselves more closely bound
Than ever. I believe that Tycho died
Simply of heartache for his native land.
For though he always met me with a
    smile,
Or jest upon his lips, he could not sleep

Or work, and often unawares I caught
Odd little whispered phrases on his lips
As if he talked to himself, in a kind of
   dream.
Yet I believe the clouds dispersed a little
Around his death-bed, and with that strange
   joy
Which comes in death, he saw the unchang-
   ing stars.
Christine was there.   She held him in her
   arms.
I think, too, that he knew his work was
   safe.
An hour before he died, he smiled at me,
And whispered,—what he meant I hardly
   know—
Perhaps a broken echo from the past,
A fragment of some old familiar thought,
And yet I seemed to know.   It haunts me
   still:
*'Come then, swift-footed, let me see you
   stand,*

Waiting before me, crowned with youth
  and joy;
This is the turning. Take it from my hand.
For I am ready, ready now, to fall.'"

III

KEPLER

JOHN KEPLER, from the chimney corner, watched
His wife Susannah, with her sleeves rolled
    back
Making a salad in a big blue bowl.
The thick tufts of his black rebellious
    hair
Brushed into sleek submission; his trim
    beard
Snug as the soft round body of a thrush
Between the white wings of his fan-shaped
    ruff
(His best, with the fine lace border) spoke
    of guests
Expected; and his quick grey humorous
    eyes,
His firm red whimsical pleasure-loving
    mouth,

And all those elvish twinklings of his face,
Were lit with eagerness. Only between his
    brows,
Perplexed beneath that subtle load of
    dreams,
Two delicate shadows brooded.
                              "What does it mean?
Sir Henry Wotton's letter breathed a hint
That Italy is prohibiting my book,"
He muttered. "Then, if Austria damns it
    too,
Susannah mine, we may be forced to choose
Between the truth and exile. When he
    comes,
He'll tell me more. Ambassadors, I sup-
    pose,
Can only write in cipher, while our world
Is steered to heaven by murderers and
    thieves;
But, if he'd wrapped his friendly warnings
    up
In a verse or two, I might have done more
    work

These last three days, eh, Sue?"

                    "Look, John," said she,

"What beautiful hearts of lettuce! Tell me
    now

How shall I mix it? Will your English
    guest

Turn up his nose at dandelion leaves

As crisp and young as these? They've just
    the tang

Of bitterness in their milk that gives a
    relish

And makes all sweet; and that's philosophy,
    John.

Now—these spring onions! Would his
    Excellency

Like sugared rose-leaves better?"

                       "He's a poet,

Not an ambassador only, so I think

He'll like a cottage salad."

                      "A poet, John!

I hate their arrogant little insect ways!

I'll put a toadstool in."

"Poets, dear heart,
Can be divided into two clear kinds,—
One that, by virtue of a half-grown brain,
Lives in a silly world of his own making,
A bubble, blown by himself, in which he
    flits
And dizzily bombinates, chanting 'I, I, I,'
For there is nothing in the heavens above
Or the earth, or hell beneath, but goes to
    swell
His personal pronoun. Bring him some
    dreadful news
His dearest friend is burned to death,—
    You'll see
The monstrous insect strike an attitude
And shape himself into one capital I,
A rubric, with red eyes. You'll see him
    use
The coffin for his pedestal, hear him mouth
His 'I, I, I' instructing haggard grief
Concerning his odd ego. Does he chirp
Of love, it's 'I, I, I' Narcissus, love,

Myself, Narcissus, imaged in those eyes;
For all the love-notes that he sounds are
made
After the fashion of passionate grasshop-
pers,
By grating one hind-leg across another.
Nor does he learn to sound that mellower
'You,'
Until his bubble bursts and leaves him
drowned,
An insect in a soap-sud.
But there's another kind, whose mind still
moves
In vital concord with the soul of things;
So that it thinks in music, and its thoughts
Pulse into natural song. A separate voice,
And yet caught up by the surrounding
choirs,
There, in the harmonies of the Universe,
Losing himself, he saves his soul alive."
"John, I'm afraid!"—

      "Afraid of what, Susannah?"—
"Afraid to put those Ducklings on to roast.

Your friend may miss his road; and, if he's
    late,
My little part of the music will be
    spoiled."—
"He won't, Susannah. Bad poets are al-
    ways late.
Good poets, at times, delay a note or two;
But all the great are punctual as the sun.
What's that? He's early! That's his
    knock, I think!"—
"The Lord have mercy, John, there's
    nothing ready!
Take him into your study and talk to him,
Talk hard. He's come an hour before his
    time;
And I've to change my dress. I'll into the
    kitchen!"

Then, in a moment, all the cottage rang
With greetings; hand grasped hand; his
    Excellency
Forgot the careful prologue he'd pre-
    pared,

And made an end of mystery. He had
    brought
A message from his wisdom-loving king
Who, hearing of new menaces to the light
In Europe, urged the illustrious Kepler
    now
To make his home in England. There,
    his thought
And speech would both be free.

                  "My friend," said Wotton,
"I have moved in those old strongholds of
    the night,
And heard strange mutterings. It is not
    many years
Since Bruno burned. There's trouble brew-
    ing too,
For one you know, I think,—the Floren-
    tine
Who made that curious optic tube."—

                       'You mean
The man at Padua, Galileo?"—

                          "Yes."

"They will not dare or need. Proof or
    disproof
Rests with their eyes."—
           "Kepler, have you not heard
Of those who, fifteen hundred years ago,
Had eyes and would not see? Eyes quickly
    close
When souls prefer the dark."—
"So be it. Other and younger eyes will see.
Perhaps that's why God gave the young a
    spice
Of devilry. They'll go look, while elders
    gasp;
And, when the Devil and Truth go hand in
    hand,
God help their enemies. You will send my
    thanks,
My grateful thanks, Sir Henry, to your
    king.
To-day I cannot answer you. I must think.
It would be very difficult. My wife
Would find it hard to leave her native land.
Say nothing yet before her."

Then, to hide
Their secret from Susannah, Kepler poured
His mind out, and the world's dead
    branches bloomed.
For, when he talked, another spring began
To which our May was winter; and, in the
    boughs
Of his delicious thoughts, like feathered
    choirs,
Bits of old rhyme, scraps from the Sabine
    farm,
Celestial phrases from the Shepherd King,
And fluttering morsels from Catullus sang.
Much was fantastic. All was touched with
    light
That only genius knows to steal from
    heaven.
He spoke of poetry, as the "flowering time
Of knowledge," called it "thought in pas-
    sionate tune
With those great rhythms that steer the
    moon and sun;

Thought in such concord with the soul of
    things
That it can only move, like tides and stars,
And man's own beating heart, and the wings
    of birds,
In law, whose service only sets them free."
Therefore it often leaps to the truth we
    seek,
Clasping it, as a lover clasps his bride
In darkness, ere the sage can light his lamp.
And so, in music, men might find the road
To truth, at many a point, where sages
    grope.
One day, a greater Plato would arise
To write a new philosophy, he said,
Showing how music is the golden clue
To all the windings of the world's dark
    maze.
Himself had used it, partly proved it, too,
In his own book,—*the Harmonies of the
World.*

'All that the years discover points one way
To this great ordered harmony," he said,
"Revealed on earth by music. Planets
    move
In subtle accord like notes of one great
    song
Audible only to the Artificer,
The Eternal Artist. There's no grief, no
    pain,
But music—follow it simply as a clue,
A microcosmic pattern of the whole—
Can show you, somewhere in its golden
    scheme,
The use of all such discords; and, at last,
Their exquisite solution. Then darkness
    breaks
Into diviner light, love's agony climbs
Through death to life, and evil builds up
    heaven.
Have you not heard, in some great sym-
    phony,
Those golden mathematics making clear

The victory of the soul? Have you not
   heard
The very heavens opening?

                      Do those fools
Who thought me an infidel then, still smile
   at me
For trying to read the stars in terms of
   song,
Discern their orbits, measure their dis-
   tances,
By musical proportions? Let them smile,
My folly at least revealed those three great
   laws;
Gave me the golden vases of the Egyptians,
To set in the great new temple of my God
Beyond the bounds of Egypt.

                  They will forget
My methods, doubtless, as the years go by,
And the world's wisdom shuts its music out.
The dust will gather on all my harmonies;
Or scholars turn my pages listlessly,
Glance at the musical phrases, and pass on,

Not troubling even to read one Latin page.
Yet they'll accept those great results as
    mine.
I call them mine. How can I help exulting,
Who climbed my ladder of music to the
    skies
And found, by accident, let them call it so,
Or by the inspiration of that Power
Which built His world of music, those
    three laws:—
First, how the speed of planets round the
    sun
Bears a proportion, beautifully precise
As music, to their silver distances;
Next, that although they seem to swerve
    aside
From those plain circles of old Copernicus
Their paths were not less rhythmical and
    exact,
But followed always that most exquisite
    curve
In its most perfect form, the pure ellipse;

Third, that although their speed from point
    to point
Appeared to change, their radii always
    moved
Through equal fields of space in equal
    times.
Was this my infidelity, was this
Less full of beauty, less divine in truth,
Than their dull chaos? You, the poet will
    know
How, as those dark perplexities grew
    clear,
And old anomalous discords changed to
    song,
My whole soul bowed and cried, *Almighty
    God*
*These are Thy thoughts, I am thinking
    after Thee!*
I hope that Tycho knows. I owed so much
To Tycho Brahe; for it was he who built
The towers from which I hailed those three
    great laws.

How strange and far away it all seems now.
The thistles grow upon that little isle
Where Tycho's great Uraniborg once was.
Yet, for a few sad years, before it fell
Into decay and ruin, there was one
Who crept about its crumbling corridors,
And lit the fire of memory on its hearth."—
Wotton looked quickly up, "I think I have
        heard
Something of that. You mean poor Jeppe,
        his dwarf.
Fynes Moryson, at the Mermaid Inn one
        night
Showed a most curious manuscript, a scrawl
On yellow parchment, crusted here and
        there
With sea-salt, or the salt of those thick
        tears
Creatures like Jeppe, the crooked dwarf,
        could weep.
It had been found, clasped in a crooked
        hand,
Under the cliffs of Wheen, a crooked hand

That many a time had beckoned to passing
    ships,
Hoping to find some voyager who would
    take
A letter to its master.
                The sailors laughed
And jeered at him, till Jeppe threw stones
    at them.
And now Jeppe, too, was dead, and one
    who knew
Fynes Moryson, had found him, and
    brought home
That curious crooked scrawl. Fynes Eng-
    lished it
Out of its barbarous Danish. Thus it ran:
'Master, have you forgotten Jeppe, your
    dwarf,
Who used to lie beside the big log-fire
And feed from your own hand? The hall
    is dark,
There are no voices now,—only the wind
And the sea-gulls crying round Uraniborg.
I too am crying, Master, even I,

THE TORCH-BEARERS

Because there is no fire upon the hearth,
No light in any window. It is night,
And all the faces that I knew are gone.

Master, I watched you leaving us. I saw
The white sails dwindling into sea-gull's
    wings,
Then melting into foam, and all was dark.
I lay among the wild flowers on the cliff
And dug my nails into the stiff white chalk
And called you, Tycho Brahe. You did
    not hear;
But gulls and jackdaws, wheeling round
    my head,
Mocked me with *Tycho Brahe,* and *Tycho
Brahe!*

You were a great magician, Tycho Brahe;
And, now that they have driven you away,
I, that am only Jeppe,—the crooked dwarf,
You used to laugh at for his matted hair,
And head too big and heavy—take your
    pen

Here in your study. I will write it down
And send it by a sailor to the King
Of Scotland, and who knows, the mouse
    that gnawed
The lion free, may save you, Tycho
    Brahe.' "
"He is free now," said Kepler, "had he
    lived
He would have sent for Jeppe to join him
    there
At Prague. But death forestalled him,
    and your King.
The years in which he watched that planet
    Mars,
His patient notes and records, all were
    mine;
And, mark you, had he clipped or trimmed
    one fact
By even a hair's-breadth, so that his re-
    sults
Made a pure circle of that planet's path
It might have baffled us for an age and
    drowned

[119]

All our new light in darkness.   But he held
To what he saw.   He might so easily,
So comfortably have said, 'My instruments
Are crude and fallible.   In so fine a point
Eyes may have erred, too.   Why not ac-
      quiesce?
Why mar the tune, why dislocate a world,
For one slight clash of seeming fact with
      faith?'
But no, though stars might swerve, he held
      his course,
Recording only what his eyes could see
Until death closed them.
            Then, to his results,
I added mine and saw, in one wild gleam,
Strange as the light of day to one born
      blind,
A subtler concord ruling them and heard
Profounder tones of harmony resolve
Those broken melodies into song again."—
"Faintly and far away, I, too, have seen
In music, and in verse, that golden clue

Whereof you speak," said Wotton. "In
    all true song,
There is a hidden logic. Even the rhyme
That, in bad poets, wrings the neck of
    thought,
Is like a subtle calculus to the true,
An instrument of discovery. It reveals
New harmonies, new analogies. It links
Far things and near, not in unnatural
    chains,
But in those true accords which still escape
The plodding reason, yet unify the world.
I caught some glimpses of this mystic
    power
In verses of your own, that elegy
On Tycho, and that great quatrain of
    yours—
I cannot quite recall the Latin words,
But made it roughly mine in words like
    these:

'I know that I am dust, and daily die;

[121]

Yet, as I trace those rhythmic spheres at
   night,
I stand before the Thunderer's throne on
   high
And feast on nectar in the halls of light.'

My version lacks the glory of your lines
But . . ."
                    "Mine too was a version,"
      Kepler laughed,
"Turned into Latin from old Ptolemy's
      Greek;
For, even in verse, half of the joy, I think,
Is just to pass the torch from hand to hand
An undimmed splendour.   But, last night,
      I tried
Some music all my own.   I had a dream
That I was wandering in some distant
      world.
I have often dreamed it.   Once it was the
      moon.
I wrote that down in prose.   When I am
      dead,

It may be printed. This was a fairer
    dream:
For I was walking in a far-off spring
Upon the planet, Venus. Only verse
Could spread true wings for that delicious
    world;
And so I wrote it—for no eyes but mine,
Or 'twould be seized on, doubtless, as fresh
    proof
Of poor old Kepler's madness."—

                  "Let me hear,
Madman to madman; for I, too, write
    verse."
Then Kepler, in a rhythmic murmur,
    breathed
His rich enchanted memories of that
    dream:

"Beauty burned before me
    Swinging a lanthorn through that
        fragrant night.
  I followed a distant singing,
    And a dreaming light

[123]

THE TORCH-BEARERS

How she led me, I cannot tell
To that strange world afar,
Nor how I walked, in that wild glen
Upon the sunset star.

Wingèd creatures floated
Under those rose-red boughs of violet
bloom,
With delicate forms unknown on Earth
'Twixt irised plume and plume;
Human-hearted, angel-eyed,
And crowned with unknown flowers;
For nothing in that enchanted world
Followed the way of ours.

Only I saw that Beauty,
On Hesper, as on earth, still held com-
mand;
And though, as one in slumber,
I roamed that radiant land,
With all these earth-born senses sealed
To what the Hesperians knew,
The faithful lanthorn of her law

Was mine on Hesper too.

Then, half at home with wonder,
    I saw strange flocks of flowers like
        birds take flight;
Great trees that burned like opals
    To lure their loves at night;
Dark beings that could move in realms
    No dream of ours has known.
Till these became as common things
    As men account their own.

Yet, when that lanthorn led me
    Back to the world where once I
        thought me wise;
I saw, on this my planet,
What souls, with awful eyes.
Hardly I dared to walk her fields
    As in that strange re-birth
·I looked on those wild miracles
    The birds and flowers of earth."

Silence a moment held them, loth to break
The spell of that strange dream,

"One proof the more,"
Said Wotton at last, "that songs can mount
    and fly
To truth; for this fantastic vision of yours
Of life in other spheres, awakes in me,
Either that slumbering knowledge of Soc-
    rates,
Or some strange premonition that the years
Will prove it true.   This music leads us far
From all our creeds, except that faith in law.
Your quest for knowledge—how it rests on
    that!
How sure the soul is that if truth destroy
The temple, in three days the truth will
    build
A nobler temple; and that order reigns
In all things.   Even your atheist builds his
    doubt
On that strange faith; destroys his heaven
    and God
In absolute faith that his own thought is
    true
To law, God's lanthorn to our stumbling
    feet;

And so, despite himself, he worships
    God,
For where true souls are, there are God
    and heaven."—

"It is an ancient wisdom. Long ago,"
Said Kepler, "under the glittering Eastern
    sky,
The shepherd king looked up at those great
      stars,
Those ordered hosts, and cried *Cœli narrant
Gloriam Dei!*
          .Though there be some to-day
Who'd ape Lucretius, and believe them-
    selves
Epicureans, little they know of him
Who, even in utter darkness, bowed his
    head,
To something nobler than the gods of
    Rome
Reigning beyond the darkness.
                They accept
The law, the music of these ordered worlds;
And straight deny the law's first postulate,

That out of nothingness nothing can be
  born,
Nor greater things from less. Can music
  rise
By chance from chaos, as they said that star
In Serpentarius rose? I told them, then,
That when I was a boy, with time to spare,
I played at anagrams. Out of my Latin
  name
Johannes Keplerus came that sinister phrase
Serpens in akuleo. Struck by this,
I tried again, but trusted it to chance.
I took some playing cards, and wrote on
  each
One letter of my name. Then I began
To shuffle them; and, at every shuffle, I
  read
The letters, in their order, as they came,
To see what meaning chance might give to
  them.
Wotton, the gods and goddesses must have
  laughed
To see the weeks I lost in studying chance;
  [128]

For had I scattered those cards into the
    black
Epicurean eternity, I'll swear
They'd still be playing at leap-frog in the
    dark,
And show no glimmer of sense. And yet—
    to hear
Those wittols talk, you'd think you'd but
    to mix
A bushel of good Greek letters in a sack
And shake them roundly for an age or so,
To pour the Odyssey out.

                  At last, I told,
Those disputants what my wife had said.
    One night
When I was tired and all my mind a-dust
With pondering on their atoms, I was
    called
To supper, and she placed before me there
A most delicious salad. 'It would appear,'
I thought aloud, 'that if these pewter dishes,
Green hearts of lettuce, tarragon, slips of
    thyme,

[129]

Slices of hard boiled egg, and grains of salt.
With drops of water, vinegar and oil,
Had in a bottomless gulf been flying about
From all eternity, one sure certain day
The sweet invisible hand of Happy Chance
Would serve them as a salad.'
                'Likely enough,'
My wife replied, 'but not so good as mine,
Nor so well dressed.' "
           They laughed.   Susannah's voice
Broke in, "I've made a better one.   The
   receipt
Came from the *Golden Lion*.   I have
   dished
Ducklings and peas and all.   Come, John,
   say grace."

IV

GALILEO

I

*(Celeste, in the Convent at Arcetri, writes to her old
lover at Rome.)*

M Y friend, my dearest friend, my
own dear love,
I, who am dead to love, and see around me
The funeral tapers lighted, send this cry
Out of my heart to yours, before the end.
You told me once you would endure the
rack
To save my heart one pang. O, save it
now!
Last night there came a dreadful word
from Rome
For my dear lord and father, summoning
him

[131]

Before the inquisitors there, to take his
    trial
At threescore years and ten. There is a
    threat
Of torture, if his lips will not deny
The truth his eyes have seen.
                     You know my father,
You know me, too. You never will believe
That he and I are enemies of the faith.
Could I, who put away all earthly love,
Deny the Cross to which I nailed this
    flesh?
Could he, who, on the night when all those
    heavens
Opened above us, with their circling
    worlds,
Knelt with me, crushed beneath that
    weight of glory,
Forget the Maker of that glory now?
You'll not believe it. Neither would the
    Church,
Had not his enemies poisoned all the
    springs

And fountain-heads of truth. It is not
   Rome
That summons him, but Magini, Sizy,
   Scheiner,
Lorini, all the blind, pedantic crew
That envy him his fame, and hate his
   works
For dwarfing theirs.
           Must such things always be
When truth is born?
Only five nights ago we walked together,
My father and I, here in the Convent
   garden;
And, as the dusk turned everything to
   dreams,
We dreamed together of his work well
   done
And happiness to be. We did not dream
That even then, muttering above his book,
His enemies, those enemies whom the
   truth
Stings into hate, were plotting to destroy
   him.

Yet something shadowed him. I recall
    his words—
"The grapes are ripening. See, Celeste,
    how black
And heavy. We shall have good wine
    this year,"—
"Yes, all grows ripe," I said, "your life-
    work, too,
Dear father. Are you happy now to know
Your book is printed, and the new world
    born?"
He shook his head, a little sadly, I
    thought.
"Autumn's too full of endings. Fruits
    grow ripe
And fall, and then comes winter."
                  "Not for you!
Never," I said, "for those who write their
    names
In heaven. Think, father, through all
    ages now
No one can ever watch that starry sky
Without remembering you. Your fame..."

And there

He stopped me, laid his hand upon my
    arm,

And standing in the darkness with dead
    leaves

Drifting around him, and his bare grey
    head

Bowed in complete humility, his voice

Shaken and low, he said like one in prayer,

"Celeste, beware of that.   Say truth, not
    fame.

If there be any happiness on earth,

It springs from truth alone, the truth we
    live

In act and thought.   I have looked up
    there and seen

Too many worlds to talk of fame on earth.

Fame, on this grain of dust among the
    stars,

The trumpet of a gnat that thinks to halt

The great sun-clusters moving on their way

In silence!   Yes, that's fame, but truth,
    Celeste,

Truth and its laws are constant, even up
    there;
That's where one man may face and fight
    the world.
His weakness turns to strength. He is
    made one
With universal forces, and he holds
The password to eternity.
Gate after gate swings back through all
    the heavens.
No sentry halts him, and no flaming sword.
Say truth, Celeste, not fame."
                    "No, for I'll say
A better word," I told him. "I'll say
    love."
He took my face between his hands and
    said—
His face all dark between me and the
    stars—
"What's love, Celeste, but this dear face
    of truth
Upturned to heaven."
              He left me, and I heard,

Some twelve hours later, that this man
    whose soul
Was dedicate to Truth, was threatened
    now
With torture, if his lips did not deny
The truth he loved.
            I tell you all these things
Because to help him, you must understand
    him;
And even you may doubt him, if you hear
Only those plausible outside witnesses
Who never heard his heart-beats as have I.
So let me tell you all—his quest for truth,
And how this hate began.
            Even from the first,
He made his enemies of those almost-
    minds
Who chanced upon some new thing in the
    dark
And could not see its meaning, for he saw,
Always, the law illumining it within.
So when he heard of that strange optic-
    glass

Which brought the distance near, he
    thought it out
By reason, where that other hit upon it
Only by chance. He made his telescope;
And O, how vividly that day comes back,
When in their gorgeous robes the Senate
    stood
Beside him on that high Venetian tower,
Scanning the bare blue sea that showed
    no speck
Of sail. Then, one by one, he bade them
    look;
And one by one they gasped, "a miracle."
Brown sails and red, a fleet of fishing
    boats,
See how the bright foam bursts around
    their bows!
See how the bare-legged sailors walk the
    decks!
Then, quickly looking up, as if to catch
The vision, ere it tricked them, all they
    saw
Was empty sea again.

WATCHERS OF THE SKY

                       Many believed
That all was trickery, but he bade them
    note
The colours of the boats, and count their
    sails.
Then, in a little while, the naked eye
Saw on the sky-line certain specks that
    grew,
Took form and colour; and, within an
    hour,
Their magic fleet came foaming into port.
Whereat old senators, wagging their white
    beards,
And plucking at golden chains with stiff
    old claws
Too feeble for the sword-hilt, squeaked at
    once:
"This glass will give us great advantages
In time of war."
                  War, war, O God of love,
Even amidst their wonder at Thy world,
Dazed with new beauty, gifted with new
    powers,

These old men dreamed of blood. This
    was the thought
To which all else must pander, if he hoped
Even for one hour to see those dull eyes
    blaze
At his discoveries.
"Wolves," he called them, "wolves";
And yet he humoured them. He stooped
    to them.
Promised them more advantages, and
    talked
As elders do to children. You may call it
Weakness, and yet could any man do
    more,
Alone, against a world, with such a trust
To guard for future ages? All his life
He has had some weanling truth to guard,
    has fought
Desperately to defend it, taking cover
Wherever he could, behind old fallen trees
Of superstition, or ruins of old thought.
He has read horoscopes to keep his work
Among the stars in favour with his prince.

WATCHERS OF THE SKY

I tell you this that you may understand
What seems inconstant in him. It may be
That he was wrong in these things, and
    must pay
A dreadful penalty. But you must explore
His mind's great ranges, plains and lonely
    peaks
Before you know him, as I know him now.
How could he talk to children, but in
    words
That children understand? Have not
    some said
That God Himself has made His glory
    dark
For men to bear it. In his human sphere
My father has done this.
                  War was the dream
That filmed those old men's eyes. They
    did not hear
My father, when he hinted at his hope
Of opening up the heavens for mankind
With that new power of bringing far
    things near.

[141]

My heart burned as I heard him; but they
    blinked
Like owls at noonday.   Then I saw him
    turn,
Desperately,   to   humour   them,   from
    thoughts
Of heaven to thoughts of warfare.
                       Late that night
My own dear lord and father came to me
And whispered, with a glory in his face
As one who has looked on things too
    beautiful
To breathe aloud, "Come out, Celeste, and
    see
A miracle."
            I followed him.   He showed me,
Looking along his outstretched hand, a
    star,
A point of light above our olive-trees.
It was the star called Jupiter.   And then
He bade me look again, but through his
    glass.
I feared to look at first, lest I should see

Some wonder never meant for mortal eyes.
He too, had felt the same, not fear, but
    awe,
As if his hand were laid upon the veil
Between this world and heaven.
                         Then . . . I, too, saw,
Small as the smallest bead of mist that
    clings
To a spider's thread at dawn, the floating
    disk
Of what had been a star, a planet now,
And near it, with no disk that eyes could
    see,
Four needle-points of light, unseen before.
"The moons of Jupiter," he whispered
    low,
"I have watched them as they moved, from
    night to night;
A system like our own, although the world
Their fourfold lights and shadows make so
    strange
Must—as I think—be mightier than we
    dreamed,

A Titan planet. Earth begins to fade
And dwindle; yes, the heavens are open-
    ing now.
Perhaps up there, this night, some lonely
    soul
Gazes at earth, watches our dawning moon,
And wonders, as we wonder."
                        In that dark
We knelt together . . .
                    Very strange to see
The vanity and fickleness of princes.
Before his enemies had provoked the wrath
Of Rome against him, he had given the
    name
Of Medicean stars to those four moons
In honour of Prince Cosmo. This aroused
The court of France to seek a lasting place
Upon the map of heaven. A letter came
Beseeching him to find another star
Even more brilliant, and to call it *Henri*
After the reigning and most brilliant prince
Of France. They did not wish the family
    name

Of Bourbon. This would dissipate the
glory.
No, they preferred his proper name of
Henri.
We read it together in the garden here,
Weeping with laughter, never dreaming
then
That this, this, this, could stir the little
hearts
Of men to envy.
O, but afterwards,
The blindness of the men who thought
themselves
His enemies. The men who never knew
him,
The men that had set up a thing of straw
And called it by his name, and wished to
burn
Their image and himself in one wild fire.
Men? Were they men or children? They
refused
Even to look through Galileo's glass,

Lest seeing might persuade them. Even
    that sage,
That great Aristotelian, Julius Libri,
Holding his breath there, like a fractious
    child
Until his cheeks grew purple, and the veins
Were bursting on his brow, swore he would
    die
Sooner than look.

            And that poor monstrous babe
Not long thereafter, kept his word and
    died,
Died of his own pent rage, as I have heard.
Whereat my lord and father shook his
    head
And, smiling, somewhat sadly—oh, you
    know
That smile of his, more deadly to the false
Than even his reasoning—murmured,
    "Libri, dead,
Who called the moons of Jupiter absurd!
He swore he would not look at them from
    earth,

I hope he saw them on his way to heaven.'
Welser in Augsburg, Clavius at Rome,
Scoffed at the fabled moons of Jupiter,
It was a trick, they said.   He had made a
      glass
To fool the world with false appearances.
Perhaps the lens was flawed.   Perhaps
      his wits
Were wandering.   Anything rather than
      the truth
Which might disturb the mighty in their
      seat.
"Let Galileo hold his own opinions.
I, Clavius, will hold mine."
                              He wrote to Kepler;
"You, Kepler, are the first, whose open
      mind
And lofty genius could accept for truth
The things which I have seen.   With you
      for friend,
The abuse of the multitude will not trouble
      me.
Jupiter stands in heaven and will stand,

Though all the sycophants bark at him.

       In Pisa,

Florence, Bologna, Venice, Padua,

Many have seen the moons. These wit-
  nesses

Are silent and uncertain. Do you wonder?

Most of them could not, even when they
  saw them,

Distinguish Mars from Jupiter. Shall we
  side

With Heraclitus or Democritus?

I think, my Kepler, we will only laugh

At this immeasurable stupidity.

Picture the leaders of our college here.

A thousand times I have offered them the
  proof

Of their own eyes. They sleep here, like
  gorged snakes,

Refusing even to look at planets, moons,

Or telescope. They think philosophy

Is all in books, and that the truth is
  found

Neither in nature, nor the Universe,

[148]

But in comparing texts. How you would
    laugh
Had you but heard our first philosopher
Before the Grand Duke, trying to tear
    down
And argue the new planets out of heaven,
Now by his own weird logic and closed
    eyes
And now by magic spells."
                         How could he help
Despising them a little? It's an error
Even for a giant to despise a midge;
For, when the giant reels beneath some
    stroke
Of fate, the buzzing clouds will swoop
    upon him,
Cluster and feed upon his bleeding wounds,
And do what midges can to sting him
    blind.
These human midges have not missed
    their chance.
They have missed no smallest spot upon
    that sun.

THE TORCH-BEARERS

My mother was not married—they have
    found—
To my dear father. All his children, then,
And doubtless all their thoughts are evil,
    too;
But who that judged him ever sought to
    know
Whether, as evil sometimes wears the cloak
Of virtue, nobler virtue in this man
Might wear that outward semblance of a
    sin?
Yes, even you who love me, may believe
These thoughts are born of my own tainted
    heart;
And yet I write them, kneeling in my cell
And whisper them to One who blesses me
Here, from His Cross, upon the bare grey
    wall.
So, if you love me, bless me also, you,
By helping him. Make plain to all you
    meet
What part his enemies have played in this.

WATCHERS OF THE SKY

How some one, somehow, altered the
    command
Laid on him all those years ago, by Rome,
So that it reads to-day as if he vowed
Never to think or breathe that this round
    earth
Moves with its sister-planets round the
    sun.
'Tis true he promised not to write or speak
As if this truth were 'stablished equally
With God's eternal laws; and so he wrote
His Dialogues, reasoning for it, and against,
And gave the last word to Simplicio,
Saying that human reason must bow down
Before the power of God.
               And even this
His enemies have twisted to a sneer
Against the Pope, and cunningly declared
Simplicio to be Urban.
             Why, my friend,
There were three dolphins on the title-
    page,

Each with the tail of another in its mouth.
The censor had not seen this, and they
    swore
It held some hidden meaning. Then they
    found
The same three dolphins sprawled on all
    the books
Landini printed at his Florence press.
They tried another charge.

                I am not afraid
Of any truth that they can bring against
    him;
But, O, my friend, I more than fear their
    lies.
I do not fear the justice of our God;
But I do fear the vanity of men;
Even of Urban; not His Holiness,
But Urban, the weak man, who may resent,
And in resentment rush half-way to meet
This cunning lie with credence. Vanity!
O, half the wrongs on earth arise from
    that!

Greed, and war's pomp, all envy, and most
    hate,
Are born of that; while one dear humble
    heart,
Beating with love for man, between two
    thieves,
Proves more than all His wounds and
    miracles
Our Crucified to be the Son of God.
Say that I long to see him; that my prayers
Knock at the gates of mercy, night and day.
Urge him to leave the judgment now with
    God
And strive no more.
                  If he be right, the stars
Fight for him in their courses. Let him
    bow
His poor, dishonoured, glorious, old grey
    head
Before this storm, and then come home to
    me.
O, quickly, or I fear 'twill be too late;

THE TORCH-BEARERS

For I am dying.   Do not tell him this;
But I must live to hold his hands again,
And know that he is safe.
I dare not leave him, helpless and half
    blind,
Half father and half child, to rack and
    cord.
By all the Christ within you, save him,
    you;
And, though you may have ceased to love
    me now,
One faithful shadow in your own last hour
Shall watch beside you till all shadows die,
And heaven unfold to bless you where I
    failed.

II

(Scheiner writes to Castelli, after the Trial.)

What think you of your Galileo now,
Your hero that like Ajax should defy
The lightning?   Yesterday I saw him
    stand

Trembling before our court of Cardinals,
Trembling before the colour of their robes
As sheep, before the slaughter, at the sight
And smell of blood.   His lips could hardly
    speak,
And—mark you—neither rack, nor cord
    had touched him.
Out of the Inquisition's five degrees
Of rigor: first, the public threat of torture;
Second, the repetition of the threat
Within the torture-chamber, where we
    show
The instruments of torture to the accused;
Third, the undressing and the binding;
    fourth,
Laying him on the rack; then, fifth and
    last,
Torture, *territio realis;* out of these,
Your Galileo reached the second only,
When, clapping both his hands against his
    sides,
He whined about a rupture that forbade

These extreme courses. Great heroic soul
Dropped like a cur into a sea of terror,
He sank right under. Then he came up
    gasping,
Ready to swear, deny, abjure, recant,
Anything, everything! Foolish, weak, old
    man,
Who had been so proud of his discoveries,
And dared to teach his betters. How we
    grinned
To see him kneeling there and whispering,
    thus,
Through his white lips, bending his old
    grey head:
"I, Galileo Galilei, born
A Florentine, now seventy years of age,
Kneeling before you, having before mine
    eyes,
And touching with my hands the Holy
    Gospels,
Swear that I always have believed, do
    now,
And always will believe what Holy Church

Has held and preached and taught me to
*   believe;*
And now, whereas I rightly am accused,
Of heresy, having falsely held the sun
To be the centre of our Universe,
And also that this earth is not the centre,
But moves;
I most illogically desire
Completely to expunge this dark suspicion,
So reasonably conceived. I now abjure,
Detest and curse these errors; and I swear
That should I know another, friend or
*   foe,*
Holding the selfsame heresy as myself,
I will denounce him to the Inquisitor
In whatsoever place I chance to be.
So help me God, and these His Holy
*   Gospels,*
Which with my hands I touch."
                                You will observe
His promise to denounce.   Beware, Cas-
    telli!
What think you of your Galileo now?

THE TORCH-BEARERS

III

*(Castelli writes, enclosing Scheiner's letter, to
Campanella.)*

What think I? This,—that he has laid
    his hands
Like Samson on the pillars of our world,
And one more trembling utterance such as
    this
Will overwhelm us all.

                  O, Campanella,
You know that I am loyal to our faith,
As Galileo too has always been.
You know that I believe, as he believes,
In the one Catholic Apostolic Church;
Yet there are many times when I could
    wish
That some blind Samson would indeed
    tear down
All this proud temporal fabric, made with
    hands,
And that, once more, we suffered with our
    Lord,

[158]

Were persecuted, crucified with Him.
I tell you, Campanella, on that day
When Galileo faced our Cardinals,
A veil was rent for me. There, in one
    flash,
I saw the eternal tragedy, transformed
Into new terms. I saw the Christ once
    more,
Before the court of Pilate. Peter there
Denied Him once again; and, as for me,
Never has all my soul so humbly knelt
To God in Christ, as when that sad old
    man
Bowed his grey head, and knelt—at seventy
    years—
To acquiesce, and shake the world with
    shame.
He shall not strive or cry! Strange, is it
    not,
How nearly Scheiner—even amidst his
    hate—
Quoted the Prophets? Do we think this
    world

[159]

So greatly bettered, that the ancient cry,
"*Despised, rejected,*" hails our God no
    more?

IV

*(Celeste writes to her father in his imprisonment at
Siena.)*

Dear father, it will seem a thousand years
Until I see you home again and well.
I would not have you doubt that all this
    time
I have prayed for you continually. I saw
A copy of your sentence. I was grieved;
And yet it gladdened me, for I found a way
To be of use, by taking on myself
Your penance. Therefore, if you fail in
    this,
If you forget it—and indeed, to save you
The trouble of remembering it—your child
Will do it for you.

           Ah, could she do more!
How willingly would your Celeste endure

[160]

A straiter prison than she lives in now
To set you free.

     "A prison," I have said;
And yet, if you were here, 'twould not be
  so.
When you were pent in Rome, I used to
  say,
"Would he were at Siena!" God fulfilled
That wish.. You are at Siena; and I now
  say
Would he were at Arcetri.

       So perhaps
Little by little, angels can be wooed
Each day, by some new prayer of mine or
  yours,
To bring you wholly back to me, and save
Some few of the flying days that yet remain.
You see, these other Nuns have each their
  friend,
Their patron Saint, their ever near *devoto,*
To whom they tell their joys and griefs;
  but I
Have only you, dear father, and if you

Were only near me,.I could want no more.
Your garden looks as if it missed your love.
The unpruned branches lean against the
    wall
To look for you.   The walks run wild with
    flowers.
Even your watch-tower seems to wait for
    you;
And, though the fruit is not so good this
    year
(The vines were hurt by hail, I think, and
    thieves
Have climbed the wall too often for the
    pears),
The crop of peas is good, and only waits
Your hand to gather it.
                         In the dovecote, too,
You'll find some plump young pigeons.
    We must make
A feast for your return.
                         In my small plot,
Here at the Convent, better watched than
    yours,

[162]

I raised a little harvest. With the price
I got for it, I had three Masses said
For my dear father's sake.

V

(*Galileo writes to his friend Castelli, after his return
to Arcetri.*)

Castelli, O Castelli, she is dead.
I found her driving death back with her
    soul
Till I should come.
              I could not even see
Her face.—These useless eyes had spent
    their power
On distant worlds, and lost that last faint
    look
Of love on earth.
             I am in the dark, Castelli,
Utterly and irreparably blind.
The Universe which once these outworn
    eyes
Enlarged so far beyond its ancient bounds

[163]

THE TORCH-BEARERS

Is henceforth shrunk into that narrow
    space
Which I myself inhabit.
                Yet I found
Even in the dark, her tears against my
    face,
Her thin soft childish arms around my
    neck,
And her voice whispering . . . love, un-
    dying love;
Asking me, at this last, to tell her true,
If we should meet again.
             Her trust in me
Had shaken her faith in what my judges
    held;
And, as I felt her fingers clutch my hand,
Like a child drowning, "Tell me the
    truth," she said,
"Before I lose the light of your dear
    face"—
It seemed so strange that dying she could
    see me

While I had lost her,—"tell me, before I
    go."
"Believe in Love," was all my soul could
    breathe.
I heard no answer. Only I felt her
    hand
Clasp mine and hold it tighter. Then she
    died,
And left me to my darkness. Could I
    guess
At unseen glories, in this deeper night,
Make new discoveries of profounder
    realms,
Within the soul? O, could I find Him
    there,
Rise to Him through His harmonies of law
And make His will my own!
                  This much, at least,
I know already, that—in some strange
    way—
His law implies His love; for, failing
    that

All grows discordant, and the primal Power
Ignobler than His children.

                      So I trust
One day to find her, waiting for me
   still,
When all things are made new.

                        I raise this torch
Of knowledge. It is one with my right
   hand,
And the dark sap that keeps it burning
   flows
Out of my heart; and yet, for all my faith,
It shows me only darkness.

                      Was I wrong?
Did I forget the subtler truth of Rome
And, in my pride, obscure the world's one
   light?
Did I subordinate to this moving earth
Our swiftlier-moving God?

                  O, my Celeste,
Once, once at least, you knew far more
   than I;
And she is dead, Castelli, she is dead.

[166]

WATCHERS OF THE SKY

VI

I was his last disciple, as you say
I went to him, at seventeen years of age,
And offered him my hands and eyes to use,
When, voicing the true mind and heart of
    Rome,
Father Castelli, his most faithful friend,
Wrote, for my master, that compassionate
    plea;
The noblest eye that Nature ever made
Is darkened; one so exquisitely dowered,
So delicate in power that it beheld
More than all other eyes in ages gone
And opened the eyes of all that are to come.
But, out of England, even then, there shone
The first ethereal promise of light
That crowns my master dead. Well I
    recall
That day of days. There was no faintest
    breath

[167]

THE TORCH-BEARERS

Among his garden cypress-trees. .They
    dreamed
Dark, on a sky too beautiful for tears,
And the first star was trembling overhead,
When, quietly as a messenger from heaven,
Moving unseen, through his own purer
    realm,
Amongst the shadows of our mortal world,
A young man, with a strange light on his
    face
Knocked at the door of Galileo's house.
His name was Milton.

                By the hand of God,
He, the one living soul on earth with power
To read the starry soul of this blind man,
Was led through Italy to his prison door.
He looked on Galileo, touched his hand . . .
O, dark, dark, dark, amid the blaze of noon,
Irrecoverably dark. . . .

                In after days,
He wrote it; but it pulsed within him then;
And Galileo rising to his feet
And turning on him those unseeing eyes

That had searched heaven and seen so
    many worlds,
Said to him, "You have found me."
Often he told me in those last sad months
Of how your grave young island poet
    brought
Peace to him, with the knowledge that, far
    off,
In other lands, the truth he had pro-
    claimed
Was gathering power.

               Soon after, death unlocked
His prison, and the city that he loved,
Florence, his town of flowers, whose gates
    in life
He was forbid to pass, received him dead.

You write to me from England, that his
    name
Is now among the mightiest in the world,
And in his name I thank you.

                   I am old;
And I was very young when, long ago,

THE TORCH-BEARERS

I stood beside his poor dishonoured grave
Where hate denied him even an epitaph;
And I have seen, slowly and silently,
His purer fame arising, like a moon
In marble on the twilight of those aisles
At Santa Croce, where the dread decree
Was read against him.

         Now, against two wrongs,
Let me defend two victims: first, the
    Church
Whom many have vilified for my master's
    doom;
And second, Galileo, whom they reproach
Because they think that in his blind old age
He might with one great eagle's glance
    have cowed
His judges, played the hero, raised his
    hands
Above his head, and posturing like a
    mummer
Cried (as one empty rumour now declares)
After his recantation—*yet, it moves!*
Out of this wild confusion, fourfold wrongs

Are heaped on both sides.—I would fain
    bring peace,
The peace of truth to both before I die;
And, as I hope, rest at my master's feet.
It was not Rome that tried to murder
    truth;
But the blind hate and vanity of man.
Had Galileo but concealed the smile
With which, like Socrates, he answered
    fools,
They would not, in the name of Christ,
    have mixed
This hemlock in his chalice.
                  O pitiful
Pitiful human hearts that must deny
Their own unfolding heavens, for one light
    word
Twisted by whispering malice.
                  Did he mean
Simplicio, in his dialogues, for the Pope?
Doubtful enough—the name was borrowed
    straight
From older dialogues.

If he gave one thought
Of Urban's to Simplicio—you know well
How composite are all characters in books,
How authors find their colours here and
there,
And paint both saints and villains from
themselves.
No matter. This was Urban. Make it
clear.
Simplicio means a simpleton. The saints
Are aroused by ridicule to most human
wrath.
Urban was once his friend. This hint of
ours
Kills all of that. And so we mortals close
The doors of Love and Knowledge on the
world.
And so, for many an age, the name of
Christ
Has been misused by man to mask man's
hate.
How should the Church escape, then? I
who loved

WATCHERS OF THE SKY

My master, know he had no truer friend
Than many of those true servants of the
    Church,
Fathers and priests who, in their lowlier
    sphere,
Moved nearer than her cardinals to the
    Christ.
These were the very Rome, and held her
    keys.
Those who charge Rome with hatred of
    the light
Would charge the sun with darkness, and
    accuse
This dome of sky for all the blood-red
    wrongs
That men commit beneath it. Art and
    song
That found her once in Europe their sole
    shrine
And sanctuary absolve her from that stain.

But there's this other charge against my
    friend,

And master, Galileo. It is brought
By friends, made sharper by their pity and
    grief,
The charge that he refused his martyrdom
And so denied his own high faith.
                Whose faith,—
His friends', his Protestant followers', or
    his own?
Faced by the torture, that sublime old
    man
Was still a faithful Catholic, and his
    thought
Plunged deeper than his Protestant fol-
    lowers knew.
His aim was not to strike a blow at Rome
But to confound his enemies. He believed
As humbly as Castelli or Celeste
That there is nothing absolute but that
    Power
With which his Church confronted him.
    To this
He bowed his head, acknowledging that
    his light

Was darkness; but affirming, all the more,
That Ptolemy's light was even darker yet.
Read your own Protestant Milton, who
    derived
His mighty argument from my master's
    lips:
"Whether the sun predominant in heaven
Rise on the earth, or earth rise on the sun;
Leave them to God above; Him serve and
    fear."
Just as in boyhood, when my master
    watched
The swinging lamp in the cathedral there
At Pisa; and, by one finger on his pulse,
Found that, although the great bronze
    miracle swung
Through ever-shortening spaces, yet it
    moved
More slowly, and so still swung in equal
    times;
He straight devised another boon to man,
Those pulse-clocks which by many a
    fevered bed

Our doctors use; dreamed of that, time-
    piece, too,
Whose punctual swinging pendulum on
    earth
Measures the starry periods, and to-day
Talks peacefully to children by the fire
Like an old grandad full of ancient tales,
Remembering endless ages, and foretelling
Eternities to come; but, all the while
There, in the dim cathedral, he knew
    well,
That dreaming youngster, with his tawny
    mane
Of red-gold hair, and deep ethereal eyes,
What odorous clouds of incense round him
    rose;
Was conscious in the dimness, of great
    throngs
Kneeling around him; shared in his own
    heart
The music and the silence and the cry,
O, salutaris hostia!—so now,
There was no mortal conflict in his mind

Between his dream-clocks and things abso-
    lute,
And one far voice, most absolute of all,
Feeble with suffering, calling night and day
"Return, return," the voice of his Celeste.
All these things co-existed, and the less
Were comprehended, like the swinging
    lamp,
Within that great cathedral of his soul.
Often he bade me, in that desolate house
Il Giojello, of old a jewel of light,
Read to him one sad letter, till he knew
The most of it by heart, and while he
    walked
His garden, leaning on my arm, at times
I think he quite forgot that I was there;
For he would quietly murmur it to him-
    self,
As if she had sent it, half an hour ago:
"Now, with this little winter's gift of
    fruit
I send you, father, from our southward
    wall,

[177]

Our convent's rarest flower, a Christmas
　　rose.
At this cold season, it should please you
　　much,
Seeing how rare it is; but, with the rose,
You must accept its thorns, which bring
　　to mind
Our Lord's own bitter Passion. Its green
　　leaves
Image the hope that through His Passion
　　we,
After this winter of our mortal life,
May find the beauty of an eternal spring
In heaven."
Praise me the martyr, out of whose agonies
Some great new hope is born, but not the
　　fool
Who starves his heart to prove what eyes
　　can see
And intellect confirm throughout the
　　world.
Why must he follow the idiot schoolboy
　　code,

Torture his soul to reinforce the sight
Of those that closed their eyes and would
    not see.
To your own men of science, fifty turns
Of the thumbscrew would not prove that
    earth revolved.
Call it Italian subtlety if you will,
I say his intricate cause could not be won
By blind heroics. Much that his enemies
    challenged
Was not yet wholly proven, though his
    mind
Had leapt to a certainty. He must leave
    the rest
To those that should come after, swift and
    young,—
Those runners with the torch for whom he
    longed
As his deliverers. Had he chosen death
Before his hour, his proofs had been
    obscured
For many a year. His respite gave him
    time

To push new pawns out, in the blindfold
    play
Of those last months, and checkmate, not
    the Church
But those that hid behind her. He be-
    lieved
His truth was all harmonious with her
    own.
How could he choose between them?
    Must he die
To affirm a discord that himself denied?
On many a point, he was less sure than we:
But surer far of much that we forget.
The movements that he saw he could but
    judge
By some fixed point in space. He chose
    the sun.
Could this be absolute? Could he then be
    sure
That this great sun did not with all its
    worlds
Move round a deeper centre? What
    became

Of your Copernicus then? Could he be
    sure
Of any unchanging centre, whence to
    judge
This myriad-marching universe, but one—
The absolute throne of God.

                        Affirming this
Eternal Rock, his own uncertainties
Became more certain, and although his
    lips
Breathed not a syllable of it, though he
    stood
Silent as earth that also seemed so still,
The very silence thundered, *yet it moves!*

He held to what he knew, secured his
    work
Through feeble hands like mine, in other
    lands,
Not least in England, as I think you know.
For, partly through your poet, as I believe,
When his great music rolled upon your
    skies,

THE TORCH-BEARERS

New thoughts were kindled in the general
    mind.
'Twas at Arcetri that your Milton gained
The first great glimpse of his celestial
    realm.
Picture him,—still a prisoner of our light,
Closing his glorious eyes—that in the dark,
He might behold this wheeling universe,—
The planets gilding their ethereal horns
With sun-fire. Many a pure immortal
    phrase
In his own work, as I have pondered it,
Lived first upon the lips of him whose
    eyes
Were darkened first,—in whom, too, Milton
    found
That Samson Agonistes, not himself,
As many have thought, but my dear master
    dead.
These are a part of England's memories
    now,
The music blown upon her sea-bright air
When, in the year of Galileo's death,

WATCHERS OF THE SKY

Newton, the mightiest of the sons of light,
Was born to lift the splendour of this torch
And carry it, as I heard that Tycho said
Long since to Kepler, "carry it out of
    sight,
Into the great new age I must not know,
Into the great new realm I must not tread."

V

NEWTON

I

"IF I saw farther, 'twas because I stood
   On giant shoulders," wrote the king of
      thought,
Too proud of his great line to slight the
      toils
Of his forebears. He turned to their dim
      past,
Their fading victories and their fond de-
      feats,
And knelt as at an altar, drawing all
Their strengths into his own; and so went
      forth
With all their glory shining in his face,
To win new victories for the age to come.

So, where Copernicus had destroyed the
    dream
We called our world; where Galileo
    watched
Those ancient firmaments melt, a thin
    blue smoke
Into a vaster night; where Kepler heard
Only stray fragments, isolated chords
Of that tremendous music which should
    bind
All things anew in one, Newton arose
And carried on their fire.
                Around him reeled
Through lingering fumes of hate and clouds
    of doubt,
Lit by the afterglow of the Civil War,
The dissolute throngs of that Walpurgis
    night
Where all the cynical spirits that deny
Danced with the vicious lusts that drown
    the soul
In flesh too gross for Circe or her
    swine.

But, in his heart, he heard one instant
    voice.
"On with the torch once more, make all
    things new,
Build the new heaven and earth, and save
    the world."

Ah, but the infinite patience, the long
    months
Lavished on tasks that, to the common eye,
Were insignificant, never to be crowned
With great results, or even with earth's
    rewards.
Could Rembrandt but have painted him,
    in those hours
Making his first analysis of light
Alone, there, in his darkened Cambridge
    room
At Trinity! Could he have painted, too,
The secret glow, the mystery, and the
    power,
The sense of all the thoughts and unseen
    spires

That soared to heaven around him!
　　　　　　　　　　He stood there,
Obscure, unknown, the shadow of a man
In darkness, like a grey dishevelled ghost,
—Bare-throated, down at heel, his last
　　night's supper
Littering his desk, untouched; his glim-
　　mering face,
Under his tangled hair, intent and still,—
Preparing our new universe.
　　　　　　　　　　He caught
The sunbeam striking through that bullet-
　　hole
In his closed shutter—a round white spot
　　of light
Upon a small dark screen.
　　　　　　　　　　He interposed
A prism of glass. He saw the sunbeam
　　break
And spread upon the screen its rainbow
　　band
Of disentangled colours, all in scale
Like notes in music; first, the violet ray,

THE TORCH-BEARERS

Then indigo, trembling softly into .blue;
Then green and yellow, quivering side by
    side;
Then orange, mellowing richly into red.
Then, in the screen, he made a small
    round hole
Like to the first; and through it passed
    once more
Each separate coloured ray. He let it
    strike
Another prism of glass, and saw each hue
Bent at a different angle from its path,
The red the least, the violet ray the most;
But all in scale and order, all precise
As notes in music. Last, he took a lens,
And, passing through it all those coloured
    rays,
Drew them together again, remerging all.
On that dark screen, in one white spot of
    light.

So, watching, testing, proving, he resolved
The seeming random glories of our day

WATCHERS OF THE SKY

Into a constant harmony, and found
How in the whiteness of the sunlight sleep
Compounded, all the colours of the world.
He saw how raindrops in the clouds of
    heaven
Breaking the light, revealed that sevenfold
    arch
Of colours, ranged as on his own dark
    screen,
Though now they spanned the mountains
    and wild seas.
Then, where that old-world order had gone
    down
Beneath a darker deluge, he beheld
Gleams of the great new order and re-
    called
—Fraught with new meaning and a deeper
    hope—
That covenant which God made with all
    mankind
Throughout all generations: *I will set*
My bow in the cloud, that henceforth ye
    may know

THE TORCH-BEARERS

How deeper than the wreckage of your
  dreams
Abides My law, in beauty and in power.

II

 Yet for that exquisite balance of the mind,
He, too, must pay the price.   He stood
    alone
Bewildered, at the sudden assault of fools
On this, his first discovery.

                            "I have lost
The most substantial blessing of my quiet
To follow a vain shadow.

                            I would fain
Attempt no more.   So few can understand,
Or read one thought.   So many are ready
    at once
To swoop and sting.   Indeed I would
    withdraw
For ever from philosophy."   So he wrote
In grief, the mightiest mind of that new
    age.
Let those who'd stone the Roman Curia

For all the griefs that Galileo knew
Remember the dark hours that well-nigh
    quenched
The splendour of that spirit. He could
    not sleep.
Yet, with that patience of the God in man
That still must seek the Splendour whence
    it came,
Through midnight hours of mockery and
    defeat,
In loneliness and hopelessness and tears,
He laboured on. He had no power to see
How, after many years, when he was
    dead,
Out of this new discovery men should
    make
An instrument to explore the farthest stars
And, delicately dividing their white rays,
Divine what metals in their beauty burned,
Extort red secrets from the heart of Mars,
Or measure the molten iron in the sun.
He bent himself to nearer, lowlier, tasks;
And seeing, first, that those deflected rays,

Though it were only by the faintest bloom
Of colour, imperceptible to our eyes,
Must dim the vision of Galileo's glass,
He made his own new weapon of the sky,—
That first reflecting telescope which should
    hold
In its deep mirror, as in a breathless pool
The undistorted image of a star.

III

In that deep night where Galileo groped
Like a blind giant in dreams to find what
    power
Held moons and planets to their constant
    road
Through vastness, ordered like a moving
    fleet;
What law so married them that they could
    not clash
Or sunder, but still kept their rhythmic
    pace
As if those ancient tales indeed were true

And some great angel helmed each gliding
    sphere;
Many had sought an answer. Many had
    caught
Gleams of the truth; and yet, as when a
    torch
Is waved above a multitude at night,
And shows wild streams of faces, all con-
    fused,
But not the single law that knits them all
Into an ordered nation, so our skies
For all those fragmentary glimpses, whirled
In chaos, till one eagle-spirit soared,
Found the one law that bound them all
    in one,
And through that awful unity upraised
The soul to That which made and guides
    them all.

Did Newton, dreaming in his orchard
    there
Beside the dreaming Witham, see the moon

Burn like a huge gold apple in the
    boughs
And wonder why should moons not fall
    like fruit?
Or did he see as those old tales declare
(Those fairy-tales that gather form and
    fire
Till, in one jewel, they pack the whole
    bright world)
A ripe fruit fall from some immortal
    tree
Of knowledge, while he wondered at what
    height
Would this earth-magnet lose its darkling
    power?
Would not the fruit fall earthward, though
    it grew
High o'er the hills as yonder brightening
    cloud?
Would not the selfsame power that plucked
    the fruit
Draw the white moon, then, sailing in the
    blue?

Then, in one flash, as light and song are
    born,
And the soul wakes, he saw it—this dark
    earth
Holding the moon that else would fly
    through space
To her sure orbit, as a stone is held
In a whirled sling; and, by the selfsame
    power,
Her sister planets guiding all their moons;
While, exquisitely balanced and controlled
In one vast system, moons and planets
    wheeled
Around one sovran majesty, the sun.

IV

Light and more light! The spark from
    heaven was there,
The flash of that reintegrating fire
Flung from heaven's altars, where all light
    is born,
To feed the imagination of mankind

With vision, and reveal all worlds in one.
But let no dreamer dream that his great
    work
Sprang, armed, like Pallas from the Thun-
    derer's brain.
With infinite patience he must test and
    prove
His vision now, in those clear courts of
    Truth
Whose absolute laws (bemocked by shal-
    lower minds
As less than dreams, less than the faithless
    faith
That fears the Truth, lest Truth should
    slay the dream)
Are man's one guide to his transcendent
    heaven;
For there's no wandering splendour in the
    soul,
But in the highest heaven of all is one
With absolute reality. None can climb
Back to that Fount of Beauty but through
    pain.

Long, long he toiled, comparing first the
    curves
Traced by the cannon-ball as it soared and
    fell
With that great curving road across the
    sky
Traced by the sailing moon.
                        Was earth a loadstone
Holding them to their paths by that dark
    force
Whose mystery men have cloaked beneath
    a name?
Yet, when he came to test and prove, he
    found
That all the great deflections of the moon,
Her shining cadences from the path
    direct,
Were utterly inharmonious with the law
Of that dark force, at such a distance act-
    ing,
Measured from earth's own centre. . . .
For three long years, Newton withheld
    his hope

THE TORCH-BEARERS

Until that day when light was brought
    from France,
New light, new hope, in one small glisten-
    ing fact,
Clear-cut as any diamond; and to him
Loaded with all significance, like the point
Of light that shows where constellations
    burn.
Picard in France—all glory to her name
Who is herself a light among all lands—
Had measured earth's diameter once more
With exquisite precision.
               To the throng,
Those few corrected ciphers, his results,
Were less than nothing; yet they changed
    the world.
For Newton seized them and, with trem-
    bling hands,
Began to work his problem out anew.
Then, then, as on the page those figures
    turned
To hieroglyphs of heaven, and he beheld
The moving moon, with awful cadences

Falling into the path his law ordained,
Even to the foot and second, his hand
    shook
And dropped the pencil.
                   "Work it out for me,"
He cried to those around him; for the
    weight
Of that celestial music overwhelmed him;
And, on his page, those burning hiero-
    glyphs
Were Thrones and Principalities and
    Powers . . .
For far beyond, immeasurably far
Beyond our sun, he saw that river of suns
We call the Milky Way, that glittering
    host
Powdering the night, each grain of solar
    blaze
Divided from its neighbour by a gulf
Too wide for thought to measure; each a
    sun
Huger than ours, with its own fleet of
    worlds,

Visible and invisible. Those bright throngs
That seemed dispersed like a defeated host
Through blindly wandering skies, now, at
    the word
Of one great dreamer, height o'er height
    revealed
Hints of a vaster order, and moved on
In boundless intricacies of harmony
Around one centre, deeper than all suns,
The burning throne of God.

V

He could not sleep. That intellect, whose
    wings
Dared the cold ultimate heights of Space
    and Time
Sank, like a wounded eagle, with dazed
    eyes
Back, headlong through the clouds to
    throb on earth.
What shaft had pierced him? That which
    also pierced

[200]

His great forebears—the hate of little men.
They flocked around him, and they flung
    their dust
Into the sensitive eyes and laughed to see
How dust could blind them.
                    If one prickling grain
Could so put out his vision and so torment
That delicate brain, what weakness! How
    the mind
That seemed to dwarf us, dwindles! Is he
    mad?
So buzzed the fools, whose ponderous
    mental wheels
Nor dust, nor grit, nor stones, nor rocks
    could irk
Even for an instant.
                    Newton could not sleep,
But all that careful malice could design
Was blindly fostered by well-meaning folly,
And great sane folk like Mr. Samuel Pepys
Canvassed his weakness and slept sound
    all night.
For little Samuel with his rosy face

Came chirping into a coffee-house one day
Like a plump robin, "Sir, the unhappy
    state
Of Mr. Isaac Newton grieves me much.
Last week I had a letter from him, filled
With strange complainings, very curious
    hints,
Such as, I grieve to say, are common
    signs
—I have observed it often—of worse to
    come.
He said that he could neither eat nor
    sleep
Because of all the embroilments he was in,
Hinting at nameless enemies. Then he
    begged
My pardon, very strangely. I believe
Physicians would confirm me in my fears.
'Tis very sad. . . . Only last night, I
    found
Among my papers certain lines composed
By—whom d'you think?—My lord of
    Halifax

WATCHERS OF THE SKY

(Or so dear Mrs. Porterhouse assured me)
Expressing, sir, the uttermost satisfaction
In Mr. Newton's talent. Sir, he wrote
Answering the charge that science would
    put out
The light of beauty, these very handsome
    lines:

'When Newton walked by Witham stream
  There fell no chilling shade
To blight the drifting naiad's dream
  Or make her garland fade.

The mist of sun was not less bright
  That crowned Urania's hair.
He robbed it of its colder light,
  But left the rainbow there.'

They are very neat and handsome, you'll
    agree.
Solid in sense as Dryden at his best,
And smooth as Waller, but with something
    more,—

That touch of grace, that airier elegance
Which only rank can give.

                'Tis very sad
That one so nobly praised should—well, no
    matter!—
I am told, sir, that these troubles all
    began
At Cambridge, when his manuscripts were
    burned.
He had been working, in his curious way,
All through the night; and, in the morning
    greyness
Went down to chapel, leaving on his desk
A lighted candle. You can imagine it,—
A sadly sloven altar to his Muse,
Littered with papers, cups, and greasy
    plates
Of untouched food. I am told that he
    would eat
His Monday's breakfast, sir, on Tuesday
    morning,
Such was his absent way!

When he returned,
He found that Diamond (his little dog
Named Diamond, for a black patch near
    his tail)
Had overturned the candle. All his work
Was burned to ashes.
         It struck him to the quick,
Though, when his terrier fawned about
    his feet,
He showed no anger. He was heard to
    say,
'O Diamond, Diamond, little do you
    know . . .'
But, from that hour, ah well, we'll say no
    more."

Halley was there that day, and spoke up
    sharply,
"Sir, there are hints and hints! Do you
    mean more?"
—"I do, sir," chirruped Samuel, mightily
    pleased

To find all eyes, for once, on his fat face.
"I fear his intellects are disordered, sir."
—"Good! That's an answer! I can deal
    with that.
But tell me first," quoth Halley, "why he
    wrote
That letter, a week ago, to Mr. Pepys."
—"Why, sir," piped Samuel, innocent of
    the trap,
"I had an argument in this coffee-house
Last week, with certain gentlemen, on the
    laws
Of chance, and what fair hopes a man
    might have
Of throwing six at dice. I happened to
    say
That Mr. Isaac Newton was my friend,
And promised I would sound him."

               "Sir," said Halley,
"You'll pardon me, but I forgot to tell
    you
I heard, a minute since, outside these
    doors,

A very modish woman of the town,
Or else a most delicious lady of fashion,
A melting creature with a bold black eye,
A bosom like twin doves; and, sir, a
    mouth
Like a Turk's dream of Paradise. She
    cooed,
'Is Mr. Pepys within?' I greatly fear
That they denied you to her!"
                              Off ran Pepys!
"A hint's a hint," laughed Halley, "and
    so to bed.
But, as for Isaac Newton, let me say,
Whatever his embroilments were, he solved
With just one hour of thought, not long
    ago
The problem set by Leibnitz as a challenge
To all of Europe.   He published his result
Anonymously, but Leibnitz, when he saw it,
Cried out, at once, old enemy as he was,
'That's Newton, none but Newton!   From
    this claw
I know the old lion, in his midnight lair.' "

THE TORCH-BEARERS

VI

(Sir Isaac Newton writes to Mrs. Vincent at
Woolthorpe.)

Your letter, on my eightieth birthday,
  wakes
Memories, like violets, in this London
  gloom.
You have never failed, for more than three-
  score years
To send these annual greetings from the
  haunts
Where you and I were boy and girl to-
  gether.
A day must come—it cannot now be
  far—
When I shall have no power to thank you
  for them,
So let me tell you now that, all my life,
They have come to me with healing in
  their wings
Like birds from home, birds from the
  happy woods

[208]

Above the Witham, where you walked
    with me
When you and I were young.
                Do you remember
Old Barley—how he tried to teach us
    drawing?
He found some promise, I believe, in you,
But quite despaired of me.
                  I treasure all
Those little sketches that you sent to me
Each Christmas, carrying each some
    glimpse of home.
There's one I love that shows the narrow
    lane
Behind the schoolhouse, where I had that
    bout
Of schoolboy fisticuffs. I have never
    known
More pleasure, I believe, than when I beat
That black-haired bully and won, for my
    reward,
Those April smiles from you.
                I see you still

Standing among the fox-gloves in the
    hedge;
And just behind you, in the field, I know
There was a patch of aromatic flowers,—
Rest-harrow, was it? Yes; their tangled
    roots
Pluck at the harrow; halt the sharp
    harrow of thought,
Even in old age. I never breathe their
    scent
But I am back in boyhood, dreaming there
Over some book, among the diligent bees,
Until you join me, and we dream together.
They called me lazy, then. Oddly enough
It was that fight that stirred my mind to
    beat
My bully at his books, and head the
    school;
Blind rivalry, at first. By such fond tricks
The invisible Power that shapes us—not
    ourselves—
Punishes, teaches, leads us gently on
Like children, all our lives, until we grasp

A sudden meaning and are born, through
  death
Into full knowledge that our Guide was
  Love.
Another picture shows those woods of ours,
Around whose warm dark edges in the
  spring
Primroses, knots of living sunlight, woke;
And, always, you, their radiant shepherdess
From Elfland, lead them rambling back
  for me,
The dew still clinging to their golden fleece,
Through these grey memory-mists.
                    Another shows
My old sun-dial.   You say that it is known
As "Isaac's dial" still.   I   took   great
  pains
To set it rightly.   If it has not shifted
'Twill mark the time long after I am
  gone;
Not like those curious water-clocks I made.
Do you remember?   They worked well at
  first;

But the least particles in the water clogged
The holes through which it dripped; and
　　so, one day,
We two came home so late that we were
　　sent
Supperless to our beds; and suffered
　　much
From the world's harshness, as we thought
　　it then.
Would God that we might taste that
　　harshness now.

I cannot send you what you've sent to me;
And so I wish you'll never thank me
　　more
For those poor gifts I have sent from
　　year to year.
I send another, and hope that you can
　　use it
To buy yourself those comforts which you
　　need
This Christmas-time.

　　　　　　　How strange it is to wake

And find that half a century has gone by,
With all our endless youth.
                        They talk to me
Of my discoveries, prate of undying fame
Too late to help me.   Anything I achieved
Was done through work and patience;
    and the men
Who sought quick roads to glory for
    themselves
Were capable of neither.   So I won
Their hatred, and it often hampered me,
Because it vexed my mind.
                        This world of ours
Would give me all, now I have ceased to
    want it;
For I sit here, alone, a sad old man,
Sipping his orange-water, nodding to sleep,
Not caring any more for aught they say,
Not caring any more for praise or blame;
But dreaming—things we dreamed of, long
    ago,
In childhood.
                        You and I had laughed away

That boy and girl affair. We were too
    poor
For anything but laughter.

                    I am old;
And you, twice wedded and twice widowed,
    still
Retain, through all your nearer joys and
    griefs,
The old affection. Vaguely our blind old
    hands
Grope for each other in this growing dark
And deepening loneliness,—to say "good-
    bye."
Would that my words could tell you all
    my heart;
But even my words grow old.

                  Perhaps these lines,
Written not long ago, may tell you
    more.
I have no skill in verse, despite the
    praise
Your kindness gave me, once; but since
    I wrote

[214]

WATCHERS OF THE SKY

Thinking of you, among the woods of
    home,
My heart was in them.   Let them turn to
    yours:

Give me, for friends, my own true folk
Who kept the very word they spoke;
  Whose quiet prayers, from day to day,
  Have brought the heavens about my way.

Not those whose intellectual pride
Would quench the only lights that guide;
  Confuse the lines 'twixt good and ill
  Then throne their own capricious will;

Not those whose eyes in mockery scan
The simpler hopes and dreams of man;
  Not those keen wits, so quick to hurt,
  So swift to trip you in the dirt.

Not those who'd pluck your mystery out,
Yet never saw your last redoubt;
  Whose cleverness would kill the song
  Dead at your heart, then prove you wrong.

[215]

THE TORCH-BEARERS

Give me those eyes I used to know
Where thoughts like angels come and go;
—Not glittering eyes, nor dimmed by
books,
But eyes through which the deep soul
looks.

Give me the quiet hands and face
That never strove for fame and place;
The soul whose love, so many a day
Has brought the heavens about my way.

VII

Was it a dream, that low dim-lighted
room
With that dark periwigged phantom of
Dean Swift
Writing, beside a fire, to one he loved,—
Beautiful Catherine Barton, once the light
Of Newton's house, and his half-sister's
child?

WATCHERS OF THE SKY

Yes, Catherine Barton, I am brave enough
To face this pale, unhappy, wistful ghost
Of our departed friendship.

                It was I
Savage and mad, a snarling kennel of sins,
"Your Holiness," as you called me, with
    that smile
Which even your ghost would quietly turn
    on me—
Who raised it up. It has no terrors, dear,
And I shall never lay it while I live.
You write to me. You think I have the
    power
To shield the fame of Newton from a lie.
Poor little ghost! You think I hold the
    keys
Not only of Parnassus, then, but hell.

There is a tale abroad that Newton owed
His public office to Lord Halifax,
Your secret lover. Coarseness, as you
    know,

Is my peculiar privilege. I'll be plain,
And let them wince who are whispering in
the dark.
They are hinting that he gained his public
post
Through you, his flesh and blood; and
that he knew
You were his patron's mistress!
Yes, I know
The coffee-house that hatched it—to be
scotched,
Nay, killed, before one snuff-box could say
"snap,"
Had not one cold malevolent face been
there
Listening,—that crystal-minded lover of
truth,
That lucid enemy of all lies,—Voltaire.
I am told he is doing much to spread the
light
Of Newton's great discoveries, there, in
France.

There's little fear that France, whose clear
  keen eyes
Have missed no morning in the realm of
  thought,
Would fail to see it; and smaller need to
  lift
A brand from hell to illume the light from
  heaven.
You fear he'll print his lie. No doubt of
  that.
I can foresee the phrase, as Halley saw
The advent of his comet,—*jolie nièce,*
Assez aimable, . . . then he'll give your
  name
As *Madame Conduit,* adding just that spice
Of infidelity that the dates admit
To none but these truth-lovers. It will be
  best
Not to enlighten him, or he'll change his
  tale
And make an answer difficult. Let him
  print

This truth as he conceives it, and you'll
    need
No more defence.
All history then shall damn his death-cold
    lie
And show you for the laughing child you
    were
When Newton won his office.

                      For yourself
You say you have no fear. Your only
    thought
Is that they'll soil his fame. Ah yes,
    they'll try,
But they'll not hurt it. For all time to
    come
It stands there, firm as marble and as pure.
They can do nothing that the sun and rain
Will not erase at last. Not even Voltaire
Can hurt that noble memory. Think of
    him
As of a viper writhing at the base
Of some great statue. Let the venomous
    tongue

Flicker against that marble as it may
It cannot wound it.
                              I am far more grieved
For you, who sit there wondering now, too
     late,
If it were some suspicion, some dark hint
Newton had heard that robbed him of his
     sleep,
And almost broke his mind up. I recall
How the town buzzed that Newton had
     gone mad.
You copy me that sad letter which he
     wrote
To Locke, wherein he begs him to forgive
The hard words he had spoken, thinking
     Locke
Had tried to embroil him, as he says, with
     women;
A piteous, humble letter.
                              Had he heard
Some hint of scandal that he could not
     breathe
To you, because he honoured you too well?

I cannot tell. His mind was greatly
    troubled
With other things. At least, you need not
    fear
That Newton thought it true. He walked
    aloof,
Treading a deeper stranger world than
    ours.
Have you not told me how he would forget
Even to eat and drink, when he was wrapt
In those miraculous new discoveries
And, under this wild maze of shadow and
    sun
Beheld—though not the Master Player's
    hand—
The keys from which His organ music
    rolls,
Those visible symphonies of wild cloud and
    light
Which clothe the invisible world for mortal
    eyes.
I have heard that Leibnitz whispered to
    the court

WATCHERS OF THE SKY

That Newton was an "atheist." Leibnitz
    knew
His audience. He could stoop to it.
                         Fools have said
That knowledge drives out wonder from
    the world;
They'll say it still, though all the dust's
    ablaze
With miracles at their feet; while Now-
    ton's laws
Foretell that knowledge one day shall be
    song,
And those whom Truth has taken to her
    heart
Find that it beats in music.
                         ven this age
Has glimmerings of it. Newton never saw
His own full victory; but at least he
    knew
That all the world was linked in one again;
And, if men found new worlds in years to
    come,
These too must join the universal song.

[223]

That's why true poets love him; and you'll
 find
Their love will cancel all that hate can do.
They are the sentinels of the House of
 Fame;
And that quick challenging couplet from
 the pen
Of Alexander Pope is answer enough
To all those whisperers round the outer
 doors.
There's Addison, too. The very spirit and
 thought
Of Newton moved to music when he wrote
The Spacious Firmament. Some keen-
 eyed age to come
Will say, though Newton seldom wrote a
 verse,
That music was his own and speaks his
 faith.

And, last, for those who doubt his faith
 in God

And man's immortal destiny, there re-
    mains
The granite monument of his own great
    work,
That dark cathedral of man's intellect,
The vast "Principia," pointing to the skies,
Wherein our intellectual king proclaimed
The task of science,—through this wilder-
    ness
Of Time and Space and false appearances,
To make the path straight from effect to
    cause,
Until we come to that First Cause of all,
The Power, above, beyond the blind
    machine,
The Primal Power, the originating Power,
Which cannot be mechanical. He affirmed
    it
With absolute certainty. Whence arises
    all
This order, this unbroken chain of law,
This human will, this death-defying love?

Whence, but from some divine transcendent Power,
Not less, but infinitely more than these,
Because it is their Fountain and their Guide.
Fools in their hearts have said, "Whence comes this Power,
Why throw the riddle back this one stage more?"
And Newton, from a height above all worlds
Answered and answers still:
        "This universe
Exists, and by that one impossible fact
Declares itself a miracle; postulates
An infinite Power within itself, a Whole
Greater than any part, a Unity
Sustaining all, binding all worlds in one.
This is the mystery, palpable here and now.
'Tis not the lack of links within the chain
From cause to cause, but that the chain exists.
That's the unfathomable mystery,

WATCHERS OF THE SKY

The one unquestioned miracle that we
    know,
Implying every attribute of God,
The ultimate, absolute, omnipresent Power,
In its own being, deep and high as heaven.
But men still trace the greater to the less,
Account for soul with flesh and dreams
    with dust,
Forgetting in their manifold world the
    One,
In whom for every splendour shining here
Abides an equal power behind the veil.
Was the eye contrived by blindly moving
    atoms,
Or the still-listening ear fulfilled with
    music
By forces without knowledge of sweet
    sounds?
Are nerves and brain so sensitively fash-
    ioned
That they convey these pictures of the
    world
Into the very substance of our life,

While That from which we came, the
    Power that made us,
Is ·drowned in blank unconsciousness of
    all?
Does it not from the things we know ap-
    pear
That there exists a Being, incorporeal,
Living, intelligent, who in infinite space,
As in His infinite sensory, perceives
Things in themselves, by His immediate
    presence
Everywhere? Of which things, we see no
    more
Than images only, flashed through nerves
    and brain
To our small sensories?
               What is all science then
But pure religion, seeking everywhere
The true commandments, and through
    many forms
The eternal power that binds all worlds in
    one?
It is man's age-long struggle to draw near

WATCHERS OF THE SKY

His Maker, learn His thoughts, discern
    His law,—
A boundless task, in whose infinitude,
As in the unfolding light and law of
    love.
Abides our hope, and our eternal joy.
I know not how my work may seem to
    others——"
So wrote our mightiest mind—"But to
    myself
I seem a child that wandering all day long
Upon the sea-shore, gathers here a shell,
And there a pebble, coloured by the wave,
While the great ocean of truth, from sky
    to sky
Stretches before him, boundless, unex-
    plored."

He has explored it now, and needs of me
Neither defence nor tribute. His own
    work
Remains his monument. He rose at last
    so near

The Power divine that none can nearer go;
None in this age! To carry on his fire
We must await a mightier age to come.

VI

WILLIAM HERSCHEL CONDUCTS

*WAS it a dream?—that crowded con-
    cert-room*
*In Bath; that sea of ruffles and laced
    coats;*
*And William Herschel, in his powdered
    wig,*
Waiting upon the platform, to conduct
*His choir and Linley's orchestra? He
    stood*
*Tapping his music-rest, lost in his own
    thoughts*
*And (did I hear or dream them?) all were
    mine:*

My periwig's askew, my ruffle stained
With grease from my new telescope!

THE TORCH-BEARERS

                        Ach, to-morrow
How Caroline will be vexed, although she
    grows
Almost as bad as I, who cannot leave
My work-shop for one evening.
                         I must give
One last recital at St. Margaret's,
And then—farewell to music.
                      Who can lead
Two lives at once?
               Yet—it has taught me much,
Thrown curious lights upon our world, to
    pass
From one life to another. Much that I
    took
For substance turns to shadow. I shall
    see
No throngs like this again; wring no more
    praise
Out of their hearts; forego that instant joy
—Let those who have not known it count
    it vain—

When human souls at once respond to
    yours.
Here, on the brink of fortune and of
    fame,
As men account these things, the moment
    comes
When I must choose between them and the
    stars;
And I have chosen.
                 Handel, good old friend,
We part to-night. Hereafter, I must
    watch
That other wand, to which the worlds keep
    time.

What has decided me? That marvellous
    night
When—ah, how difficult it will be to guide,
With all these wonders whirling through
    my brain!—
After a Pump-room concert I came home
Hot-foot, out of the fluttering sea of fans,

THE TORCH-BEARERS

Coquelicot-ribboned belles and periwigged
    beaux,
To my Newtonian telescope.
                    The design
Was his; but more than half the joy my
    own,
Because it was the work of my own hand,
A new one, with an eye six inches wide,
Better than even the best that Newton
    made.
Then, as I turned it on the *Gemini,*
And the deep stillness of those constant
    lights,
Castor and Pollux, lucid pilot-stars,
Began to calm the fever of my blood,
I saw, O, first of all mankind I saw
The disk of my new planet gliding there
Beyond our tumults, in that realm of peace.

What will they christen it? Ach—not
    Herschel, no!
Nor *Georgium Sidus,* as I once proposed;

Although he scarce could lose it, as he lost
That world in 'seventy-six.

           . Indeed, so far
From trying to tax it, he has granted me
How much?—two hundred golden pounds
    a year,
In the great name of science,—half the cost
Of one state-coach, with all those worlds
    to win!
Well—well—we must be grateful. This
    mad king
Has done far more than all the worldly-
    wise,
Who'll charge even this to madness.

                I believe
One day he'll have me pardoned for that
    . . . crime,
When I escaped—deserted, some would
    say—
From those drill-sergeants in my native
    land;
Deserted drill for music, as I now

Desert my music for the orchestral spheres.
No. This new planet is only new to man.
His majesty has done much. Yet, as my
    friend
Declared last night, "Never did monarch
    buy
Honour so cheaply"; and—he has not
    bought it.
I think that it should bear some ancient
    name,
And wear it like a crown; some deep, dark
    name,
Like *Uranus,* known to remoter gods.

How strange it seems—this buzzing con-
    cert-room!
There's Doctor Burney bowing and, behind
    him,
His fox-eyed daughter Fanny.
                        Is it a dream,
These crowding midgets, dense as cluster-
    ing bees
In some great bee-skep?

WATCHERS OF THE SKY

         Now, as I lift my wand,
A silence grips them, and the strings be-
    gin,
Throbbing. The faint lights flicker in
    gusts of sound.
Before me, glimmering like a crescent
    moon,
The dim half circle of the choir awaits
Its own appointed time.
             Beside me now,
Watching my wand, plump and immacu-
    late
From buckled shoes to that white bunch
    of lace
Under his chin, the midget tenor rises,
Music in hand, a linnet and a king.
The bullfinch bass, that other emperor,
Leans back indifferently, and clears his
    throat
As if to say, "This prelude leads to *Me!*"
While, on their own proud thrones, on
    either hand,
The sumptuously bosomed midget queens,
[237]

Contralto and soprano, jealously eye
Each other's plumage.
        Round me the music throbs
With an immortal passion.   I grow aware
Of an appalling mystery. . . . We, this
    throng
Of midgets, playing, listening, tense and
    still,
Are sailing on a midget ball of dust
We call our planet; will have sailed
    through space
Ten thousand leagues before this music
    ends.
What does it mean? Oh, God, what *can* it
    mean?—
This weird hushed ant-hill with a thousand
    eyes;
These midget periwigs; all those little
    blurs,
Tier over tier, of faces, masks of flesh,
Corruptible, hiding each its hopes and
    dreams,
Its tragi-comic dreams.

And all this throng
Will be forgotten, mixed with dust, crushed
    out,
Before this book of music is outworn
Or that tall organ crumbles. Violins
Outlast their players. Other hands may
    touch
That harpsichord; but ere this planet
    makes
Another threescore journeys round its sun,
These breathing listeners will have van-
    ished. Whither?
I watch my moving hands, and they grow
    strange!
What is it moves this body?   What am I?
How came I here, a ghost, to hear that
    voice
Of infinite compassion, far away,
Above the throbbing strings, hark! *Com-
    fort ye . . .*

If music lead us to a cry like this,
I think I shall not lose it in the skies.

[239]

I do but follow its own secret law
As long ago I sought to understand
Its golden mathematics; taught myself
The way to lay one stone upon another,
Before I dared to dream that I might
    build
My Holy City of Song. I gave myself
To all its branches. How they stared at
    me,
Those men of "sensibility," when I said
That algebra, conic sections, fluxions, all
Pertained to music. Let them stare again.
Old Kepler knew, by instinct, what I now
Desire to learn. I have resolved to leave
No tract of heaven unvisited.

                   To-night,
—The music carries me back to it again!—
I see beyond this island universe,
Beyond our sun, and all those other suns
That throng the Milky Way, far, far be-
    yond,
A thousand little wisps, faint nebulæ,
Luminous fans and milky streaks of fire;

WATCHERS OF THE SKY

Some like soft brushes of electric mist
Streaming from one bright point; others
    that spread
And branch, like growing systems; others
    discrete,
Keen, ripe, with stars in clusters; others
    drawn back
By central forces into one dense death,
Thence to be kindled into fire, reborn,
And scattered abroad once more in a del-
    icate spray
Faint as the mist by one bright dewdrop
    breathed
At dawn, and yet a universe like our own;
Each wisp a universe, a vast galaxy
Wide as our night of stars.
                The Milky Way
In which our sun is drowned, to these
    would seem
Less than to us their faintest drift of haze;
Yet we, who are borne on one dark grain
    of dust
Around one indistinguishable spark

Of star-mist, lost in one lost feather of
light,
Can by the strength of our own thought,
ascend
Through universe after universe; trace
their growth
Through boundless time, their glory, their
decay;
And, on the invisible road of law, more
firm
Than granite, range through all their
length and breadth,
Their height and depth, past, present and
to come.
So, those who follow the great Work-
master's law
From small things up to great, may one
day learn
The structure of the heavens, discern the
whole
Within the part, as men through Love see
God.

WATCHERS OF THE SKY

Oh, holy night, deep night of stars, whose
    peace
Descends upon the troubled mind like dew,
Healing it with the sense of that pure reign
Of constant law, enduring through all
    change;
Shall I not, one day, after faithful years,
Find that thy heavens are built on music,
    too,
And hear, once more, above thy throbbing
    worlds
This voice of all compassion, *Comfort ye,—*
Yes—*comfort ye, my people, saith your
    God?*

SIR JOHN HERSCHEL
REMEMBERS

TRUE type of all, from his own fa-
    ther's hand
He caught the fire; and, though he carried
    it far
Into new regions; and, from southern fields
Of yellow lupin, added host on host
To those bright armies which his father
    knew,
Surely the crowning hour of all his life
Was when, his task accomplished, he re-
    turned
A lonely pilgrim to the twilit shrine
Of first beginnings and his father's youth.
There, in the Octagon Chapel, with bared
    head

Grey, honoured for his father and himself,
He touched the glimmering keyboard,
    touched the books
Those dear lost hands had touched so long
    ago.

"Strange that these poor inanimate things
    outlast
The life that used them.
               Yes. I should like to try
This good old friend of his. You'll leave
    me here
An hour or so?"
          His hands explored the stops;
And, while the music breathed what else
    were mute,
His mind through many thoughts and
    memories ranged.
Picture on picture passed before him there
In living colours, painted on the gloom:
Not what the world acclaimed, the great
    work crowned,
But all that went before, the years of toil;

The years of infinite patience, hope, despair.
He saw the little house where all began,
His father's first resolve to explore the sky,
His first defeat, when telescopes were
found
Too costly for a music-master's purse;
And then that dogged and all-conquering
will
Declaring, "Be it so. I'll make my own,
A better than even the best that Newton
made."
He saw his first rude telescope—a tube
Of pasteboard, with a lens at either end;
And then,—that arduous growth to size
and power
With each new instrument, as his knowl-
edge grew;
And, to reward each growth, a deeper
heaven.
He saw the good Aunt Caroline's dismay
When her trim drawing-room, as by wiz-
ardry, turned

WATCHERS OF THE SKY

Into a workshop, where her brother's
    hands
Cut, ground and burnished, hour on aching
    hour,
Month after month, new mirrors of the
    sky.

Yet, while from dawn to dark her brother
    moved
Around some new-cut mirror, burnishing it,
Knowing that if he once removed his
    hands
The surface would be dimmed and must
    forego
Its heaven for ever, her quiet hands would
    raise
Food to his lips; or, with that musical
    voice
Which once—for she, too, offered her
    sacrifice—
Had promised her fame, she whiled away
    the hours

THE TORCH-BEARERS

Reading how, long ago, Aladdin raised
The djinns, by burnishing that old bat-
    tered lamp;
Or, from Cervantes, how one crazy soul
Tilting at windmills, challenged a purblind
    world.

He saw her seized at last by that same
    fire,
Burning to help, a sleepless Vestal, dowered
With lightning-quickness, rushing from
    desk to clock,
Or measuring distances at dead of night
Between the lamp-micrometer and his
    eyes.

He saw her in mid-winter, hurrying out,
A slim shawled figure through the drifted
    snow,
To help him; saw her fall with a stifled
    cry,
Gashing herself upon that buried hook,

And struggling up, out of the blood-stained
    drift,
To greet him with a smile.
                "For any soldier,
This wound," the surgeon muttered, "would
    have meant
Six weeks in hospital."
                Not six days for her!
"I am glad these nights were cloudy, and
    we lost
So little," was all she said.
                Sir John pulled out
Another stop. A little ironical march
Of flutes began to goose-step through the
    gloom.
He saw that first "success"! Ay, call it
    so!
The royal command,—the court desires to
    see
The planet Saturn and his marvellous rings
On Friday night. The skies, on Friday
    night,

[249]

Were black with clouds. "Canute me no
    Canutes,"
Muttered their new magician, and un-
    packed
His telescope. "You shall see what you
    can see."
He levelled it through a window; and
    they saw
"Wonderful! Marvellous! Glorious!
    Eh, what, what!"
A planet of paper, with a paper ring,
Lit by a lamp, in a hollow of Windsor
    Park,
Among the ferns, where Herne the Hunter
    walks,
And Falstaff found that fairies live on
    cheese.
Thus all were satisfied; while, above the
    clouds—
The thunder of the pedals reaffirmed—
The Titan planet, every minute, rolled
Three hundred leagues upon his awful
    way.

Then, through that night, the *vox humana*
    spoke
With deeper longing than Lucretius knew
When, in his great third book, the sombre
    chant
Kindled and soared on those exultant
    wings,
Praising the master's hand from which he,
    too,
—Father, discoverer, hero—caught the fire.
It spoke of those vast labours, incomplete,
But, through their incompletion, infinite
In beauty, and in hope; the task be-
    queathed
From dying hand to hand.

                  Close to his grave
Like a *memento mori* stood the hulk
Of that great weapon rusted and out-
    worn,
Which once broke down the barriers of the
    sky.
"Perrupit claustra"; yes, and bridged their
    gulfs;

For, far beyond our solar scheme, it
    showed
The law that bound our planets binding
    still
Those coupled suns which year by year he
    watched
Around each other circling.
                  Had our own
Some distant comrade, lost among the
    stars?
Should we not, one day, just as Kepler
    drew
His planetary music and its laws
From all those faithful records Tycho
    made,
Discern at last what vaster music rules
The vaster drift of stars from deep to deep;
Around what awful Poles, those wisps of
    light
Those fifteen hundred universes move?
One signal, even now, across the dark,
Declared their worlds confederate with our
    own;

WATCHERS OF THE SKY

For, carrying many secrets, which we now
Slowly decipher, one swift messenger comes
Across the abyss . . .
The light that, flashing through the im-
     measurable,
From universe to universe proclaims
The single reign of law that binds them all.
We shall break up those rays and, in their
     lines
And colours, read the history of their
     stars.
Year after year, the slow sure records grow,
Awaiting their interpreter.   They shall see
     it,
Our sons, in that far day, the swift, the
     strong,
The triumphing young-eyed runners with
     the torch.

No deep-set boundary-mark in Space or
     Time
Shall halt or daunt them.   Who that once
     has seen

How truth leads on to truth, shall ever
    dare
To set a bound to knowledge?
                  "Would that he knew"
—So thought the visitant at that shadowy
    shrine—
"Even as the maker of a song can hear
With the soul's ear, far off, the unstricken
    chords
To which, by its own inner law, it climbs,
Would that my father knew how younger
    hands
Completed his own planetary tune;
How from the planet that his own eyes
    found
The mind of man would plunge into the
    dark,
And, blindfold, find without the help of
    eyes
A mightier planet, in the depths beyond."

Then, while the reeds, with quiet melodious
    pace

Followed the dream, as in a picture passed,
Adams, the boy at Cambridge, making his
    vow
By that still lamp, alone in that deep
    night,
Beneath the crumbling battlements of St.
    John's,
To know why Uranus, uttermost planet
    known,
Moved in a rhythm delicately astray
From all the golden harmonies ordained
By those known measures of its sister-
    worlds.
Was there an unknown planet, far beyond,
Sailing through unimaginable deeps
And drawing it from its path?
                Then challenging chords
Echoed the prophecy that Sir John had
    made,
Guided by his own faith in Newton's law:
We have not found it, but we feel it trem-
    bling
Along the lines of our analysis now

THE TORCH-BEARERS

As once Columbus, from the shores of
Spain,
Felt the new continent.
           Then, in swift fugues, began
A race between two nations for the prize
Of that new world.
           Le Verrier in France,
Adams in England, each of them un-
    aware
Of his own rival, at the selfsame hour
Resolved to find it.
           Not by the telescope now!
Skies might be swept for æons ere one
    spark
Among those myriads were both found
    and seen
To move, at that vast distance round our
    sun.
They worked by faith in law alone. They
    knew
The wanderings of great Uranus, and they
    knew
The law of Newton.

WATCHERS OF THE SKY

                    By the midnight lamp,
Pencil in hand, shut in a four-walled
    room,
Each by pure thought must work his
    problem out,—
Given that law, to find the mass and place
Of that which drew their planet from his
    course.

There were no throngs to applaud them.
    Each alone,
Without the heat of conflict laboured on,
Consuming brain and nerve; for throngs
    applaud
Only the flash and tinsel of their day,
Never the quiet runners with the torch.
Night after night they laboured. Line on
    line
Of intricate figures, moving all in law,
They marshalled. Their long columns
    formed and marched
From battle to battle, and no sound was
    heard

Of victory or defeat. They marched
    through snows
Bleak as the drifts that broke Napoleon's
    pride
And through a vaster desert. They drilled
    their hosts
With that divine precision of the mind
To which one second's error in a year
Were anarchy, that precision which is felt
Throbbing through music.
               Month on month they toiled,
With worlds for ciphers. One rich autumn
    night
Brooding over his figures there alone
In Cambridge, Adams found them moving
    all
To one solution. To the unseeing eye
His long neat pages had no more to tell
Than any merchant's ledger, yet they shone
With epic splendour, and like trumpets
    pealed;
Three hundred million leagues beyond the
    path

WATCHERS OF THE SKY

Of our remotest planet, drowned in night
Another and a mightier planet rolls;
In volume, fifty times more vast than earth,
And of so huge an orbit that its year
Wellnigh outlasts our nations.   Though it
*   moves*
A thousand leagues an hour, it has not
*   ranged*
Thrice through its seasons since Columbus
*   sailed,*
Or more than once since Galileo died.

He took his proofs to Greenwich.   "Sweep
    the skies
Within this limited region now," he said.
"You'll find your moving planet.   I'm
    not more
Than one degree in error."
                        He left his proofs;
But Airy, king of Greenwich, looked
    askance
At unofficial genius in the young,
And pigeon-holed that music of the spheres.

Nine months he waited till Le Verrier, too,
Pointed to that same region of the sky.
Then Airy, opening his big sleepy lids,
Bade Challis use his telescope,—too late,
To make that honour all his country's own;
For all Le Verrier's proofs were now with
    Galle
Who, being German, had his star-charts
    ready
And, in that region, found one needle-
    point
Had moved. A monster planet!
                    Honour to France!
Honour to England, too, the cry began,
Who found it also, though she drowsed at
    Greenwich.
So—as the French said, with some sting
    in it—
"We gave the name of Neptune to our
    prize
Because our neighbour England rules the
    sea."

"Honour to all," say we; for, in these
    wars,
Whoever wins a battle wins for all.
But, most of all, honour to him who found
The law that was a lantern to their feet,—
Newton, the first whose thought could soar
    beyond
The bounds of human vision and declare,
"Thus saith the law of Nature and of God
Concerning things invisible."
                This new world
What was it but one harmony the more
In that great music which himself had
    heard,—
The chant of those reintegrated spheres
Moving around their sun, while all things
    moved
Around one deeper Light, revealed by law,
Beyond all vision, past all understanding,
Yet darkly shadowed forth for dreaming
    men
On earth in music . . .

THE TORCH-BEARERS

          Music, all comes back
To music in the end.
             Then, in the gloom
Of the Octagon Chapel, the dreamer lifted
    up
His face, as if to all those great forebears.
The quivering organ rolled upon the dusk
His dream of that new symphony,—the sun
Chanting to all his planets on their way
While, stop to stop replying, height o'er
    height,
His planets answered, voices of a dream:

THE SUN

Light, on the far faint planets that attend
    me!
  Light! But for me—the fury and the
    fire.
My white-hot maelstroms, the red storms
    that rend me
  Can yield them still the harvest they
    desire.

WATCHERS OF THE SKY

I kiss with light their sunward-lifted faces.
  With dew-drenched flowers I crown their
    dusky brows.
They praise me, lightly, from their pleasant
    places.
  Their birds belaud me, lightly, from
    their boughs.

And men, on lute and lyre, have breathed
    their pleasure.
  They have watched Apollo's golden
    chariot roll;
Hymned his bright wheels, but never mine
    that measure
  A million leagues of flame from Pole to
    Pole.

Like harbour-lights the stars grow wide
    before me,
  I draw my worlds ten thousand leagues
    a day.
Their far blue seas like April eyes adore
    me.

THE TORCH-BEARERS

They follow, dreaming, on my soundless
way.

How should they know, who wheel around
my burning,
What torments bore them, or what power
am I,
I, that with all those worlds around me
turning,
Sail, every hour, from sky to unplumbed
sky?

My planets, these live embers of my
passion,
These children of my hurricanes of
flame,
Flung thro' the night, for midnight to
refashion,
Praise, and forget, the splendour whence
they came.

WATCHERS OF THE SKY

The Earth

Was it a dream that, in those bright domin-
*   ions,*
*   Are other worlds that sing, with lives like*
*   mine,*
Lives that with beating hearts and broken
*   pinions*
*   Aspire and fall, half-mortal, half-divine?*

A grain of dust among those glittering
*   legions—*
*   Am I, I only, touched with joy and tears?*
O, silver sisters, from your azure regions,
*   Breathe, once again, your music of the*
*   spheres:—*

Venus

A nearer sun, a rose of light arises,
    To clothe my glens with richer clouds of
        flowers,

To paint my clouds with ever new sur-
prises
  And wreathe with mist my rosier domes
and towers;

Where now, to praise their gods, a throng
assembles
  Whose hopes and dreams no sphere but
mine has known.
On other worlds the same warm sunlight
trembles;
  But life, love, worship, these are mine
alone.

MARS

And now, as dewdrops in the dawn-light
glisten,
  Remote and cold—see—Earth and Venus
roll.
We signalled them—in music! Did they
listen?
  Could they not hear those whispers of
the soul?

WATCHERS OF THE SKY

May not their flesh have sealed that fount
    of glory,
  That pure ninth sense which told us of
    mankind?
Can some deep sleep bereave them of our
    story
  As darkness hides all colours from the
    blind?

JUPITER

I that am sailing deeper skies and dimmer,
  Twelve million leagues beyond the path
    of Mars,
Salute the sun, that cloudy pearl, whose
    glimmer
  Renews my spring and steers me through
    the stars.

Think not that I by distances am darkened.
  My months are years; yet light is in
    mine eyes.
Mine eyes are not as yours. Mine ears
    have hearkened

To sounds from earth. Five moons
enchant my skies.

SATURN

And deeper yet, like molten opal shining
My belt of rainbow glory softly streams,
And seven white moons around me inter-
twining
Hide my vast beauty in a mist of
dreams.

Huge is my orbit; and your flickering
planet
A mote that flecks your sun, that faint
white star;
Yet, in my magic pools, I still can scan it;
For I have ways to look on worlds afar.

URANUS

And deeper yet—twelve million leagues of
twilight

Divide mine empire even from Saturn's
ken.
Is there a world whose light is not as my
light,
A midget world of light-imprisoned
men?

Shut from this inner vision that hath
found me,
They hunt bright shadows, painted to
betray;
And know not that, because their night
hath drowned me,
My giants walk with gods in boundless
day.

NEPTUNE

Plunge through immensity anew and find
me.
Though scarce I see your sun,—that
dying spark—

[269]

Across a myriad leagues it still can bind
    me
  To my sure path, and steer me through
    the dark.

I sail through vastness, and its rhythms
    hold me,
  Though threescore earths could in my
    volume sleep!
Whose are the might and music that enfold
    me?
  Whose is the law that guides me thro'
    the Deep?

THE SUN

I hear their song.   They wheel around my
    burning!
  I know their orbits; but what path have I?
I that with all those worlds around me
    turning
  Sail, every hour, ten thousand leagues of
    sky?

WATCHERS OF THE SKY

My planets, these live embers of my passion,
*   And I, too, filled with music and with*
*   flame,*
Flung thro' the night, for midnight to
*   refashion,*
*   Praise and forget the Splendour whence*
*   we came.*

EPILOGUE

ONCE more upon the mountain's
    lonely height
I woke, and round me heard the sea-like
    sound
Of pine-woods, as the solemn night-wind
    washed
Through the long canyons and precipitous
    gorges
Where coyotes moaned and eagles made
    their nest.
Once more, far, far below, I saw the
    lights
Of distant cities, at the mountain's feet,
Clustered like constellations . . .
Over me, like the dome of some strange
    shrine,
Housing our great new weapon of the sky,
And moving on its axis like a moon

Glimmered the new Uraniborg.

                Shadows passed
Like monks, between it and the low grey
    walls
That lodged them, like a fortress in the
    rocks,
Their monastery of thought.

                A shadow neared me.
I heard, once more, an eager living
    voice:

"Year after year, the slow sure records
    grow.
I wish that old Copernicus could see
How, through his truth, that once dis-
    pelled a dream,
Broke the false axle-trees of heaven,
    destroyed
All central certainty in the universe,
And seemed to dwarf mankind, the spirit
    of man
Laid hold on law, that Jacob's-ladder of
    light,

[273]

And mounting, slowly, surely, step by
    step,
Entered into its kingdom and its power.
For just as Tycho's tables of the stars
Within the bound of our own galaxy
Led Kepler to the music of his laws,
So, father and son, the Herschels, with
    their charts
Of all those fire-mists, those faint nebulæ,
Those hosts of drifting universes, led
Our new discoverers to yet mightier laws
Enthroned above all worlds.
              We have not found them,
And yet—only the intellectual fool
Dreams in his heart that even his brain
    can tick
In isolated measure, a centre of law,
Amidst the whirl of universal chaos.
For law descends from law. Though all
    the spheres
Through all the abysmal depths of Space
    were blown
Like dust before a colder darker wind

Than even Lucretius dreamed, yet if one
    thought,
One gleam of law within the mind of man,
Lighten our darkness, there's a law beyond;
And even that tempest of destruction
    moves
To a lighter music, shatters its myriad
    worlds
Only to gather them up, as a shattered
    wave
Is gathered again into a rhythmic sea,
Whose ebb and flow are but the pulse of
    Life,
In its creative passion.
                   The records grow
Unceasingly, and each new grain of truth
Is packed, like radium, with whole worlds
    of light.
The eclipses timed in Babylon help us now
To clock that gradual quickening of the
    moon,
Ten seconds in a century.
                  Who that wrote

On those clay tablets could foresee his gift
To future ages; dreamed that the groping
    mind,
Dowered with so brief a life, could ever
    range
With that divine precision through the
    abyss?
Who, when that good Dutch spectacle-
    maker set
Two lenses in a tube, to read the time
Upon the distant clock-tower of his church,
Could dream of this, our hundred-inch,
    that shows
The snow upon the polar caps of Mars
Whitening and darkening as the seasons
    change?
Or who could dream when Galileo watched
His moons of Jupiter, that from their
    eclipses
And from that change in their appointed
    times,
Now late, now early, as the watching earth
Farther or nearer on its orbit rolled,

The immeasurable speed of light at last
Should be reduced to measure?

                       Could Newton dream
When, through his prism, he broke the
    pure white shaft
Into that rainbow band, how men should
    gather
And disentangle ray by delicate ray
The colours of the stars,—not only those
That burn in heaven, but those that long
    since perished,
Those vanished suns that eyes can still
    behold,
The strange lost stars whose light still
    reaches earth
Although they died ten thousand years
    ago.
Here, night by night, the innumerable
    heavens
Speak to an eye more sensitive than man's,
Write on the camera's delicate retina
A thousand messages, lines of dark and
    bright

That speak of elements unknown on earth.
How shall men doubt, who thus can read
    the Book
Of Judgment, and transcend both Space
    and Time,
Analyse worlds that long since passed away,
And scan the future, how shall they doubt
    His power
From whom their power and all creation
    came?"

I think that, when the second Herschel
    tried
Those great hexameters in our English
    tongue,
A nobler shield than ever Achilles knew
Shone through the song and made his
    echoes live:

"There he depicted the earth, and the can-
    opied sky, and the sea-waves,
There the unwearied sun, and the full-orbed
    moon in their courses,

WATCHERS OF THE SKY

All the configured stars that gem the circuit
    of heaven,
Pleiads and Hyads were there and the giant
    force of Orion,
There the revolving Bear, which the Wain
    they call, was ensculptured,
Circling on high, and in all his courses
    regarding Orion,
Sole of the starry train that descends not to
    bathe in the ocean."

A nobler shield for us, a deeper sky;
But even to us who know how far away
Those constellations burn, the wonder
    bides
That each vast sun can speed through the
    abyss
Age after age more swiftly than an eagle,
Each on its different road, alone like ours
With its own satellites; yet, since Homer
    sang,
Their aspect has not altered! All their
    flight

Has not yet changed the old pattern of the
    Wain.
The sword-belt of Orion is not sundered.
Nor has one fugitive splendour broken yet
From Cassiopeia's throne.
                    A thousand years
Are but as yesterday, even unto these.
How shall men doubt His empery over
    time
Whose dwelling is a deep so absolute
That we can only find Him in our souls.
For there, despite Copernicus, each may
    find
The centre of all things.   There He lives
    and reigns.
There infinite distance into nearness grows,
And infinite majesty stoops to dust again;
All things in little, infinite love in man . . .
Oh, beating wings, descend to earth once
    more,
And hear, reborn, the desert singer's cry:
When I consider the heavens, the work of
    Thy fingers,

WATCHERS OF THE SKY

The sun and the moon and the stars which
  Thou hast ordained,
Though man be as dust, I know Thou art
  mindful of him;
And, through Thy law, Thy light still
  visiteth him.

THE END